ANATOMY EXPLAINED

This edition published in 2015 by:

The Rosen Publishing Group, Inc.
29 East 21st Street
New York, NY 10010

Additional end matter copyright © 2015 by The Rosen
Publishing Group, Inc.

Library of Congress Cataloging-in-Publication Data

King, Abigail.
Anatomy explained/Abigail King.—First edition.
    pages cm.—(The guide for curious minds)
Includes bibliographical references and index.
ISBN 978-1-4777-8126-5 (library bound)
1. Human body—Popular works. 2. Human anatomy—Popular
works. 3. Human physiology—Popular works. I. Title.
QP38.K56 2015
612—dc23

                                        2014024520

Manufactured in the United States of America

© 2015 ELWIN STREET PRODUCTIONS www.elwinstreet.com

THE GUIDE FOR CURIOUS MINDS

ANATOMY EXPLAINED

ABIGAIL KING

ROSEN
PUBLISHING

New York

Contents

1

MAPPING OUT
THE BODY

The History of Anatomy

The question as to what lies beneath the skin has fascinated mankind since records began. Human life itself offers tantalizing glimpses: There's something beating beneath our chests, a woman's stomach expands until she has a baby, red liquid pours from painful wounds

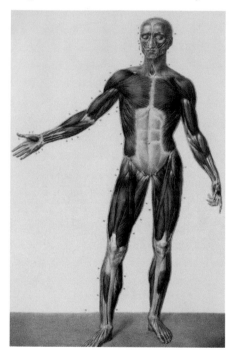

and, unless someone stops the hemorrhage, we die. So widespread is our knowledge of anatomy today—through watching TV or seeing posters and plastic models on display in doctors' waiting rooms— that it is sometimes difficult to imagine that it has taken many scientists hundreds of years to discover and understand every little piece of information now available to us.

LEFT: Besides diligent work, it took shifts in ethics and political ideas to allow research into the human body in order to produce images like this.

Ancient Myths

Just as the brightest minds on the planet once believed Earth to be flat, so many giants of science and medicine believed that women contributed nothing to the genetic makeup of their child (had they even known how to use the word "genetic"). They were clueless as to how sex led to pregnancy, bacteria and viruses to disease, and cigarette smoke to cancer. Top surgeons operated without washing their hands and academics believed that all would be well, as long as we balanced black and yellow bile, phlegm, and blood. As the medical school maxim goes: Half of what we teach you is wrong. The only trouble is, we don't yet know which half.

Anatomy and Papyrus in Ancient Egypt

The ancient Egyptian mummification process—designed to ease passage into the afterlife—contributed to world knowledge of anatomy, since organs were removed as part of the embalming process. The Edwin Smith Papyrus (so-named after the American archaeologist who purchased it in 1862) dates from around 1600 BCE and is one of the world's oldest surviving medical texts. Unlike other texts of its time, which deal principally in magic, this papyrus takes a measured, rational approach to the management of trauma. It identifies the membranes surrounding the brain and spinal cord (meninges) and makes the link between brain injury and paralysis. In short, it contains medical and anatomical knowledge that surpassed the discoveries of the ancient Greek, Hippocrates, who lived some thousand years later.

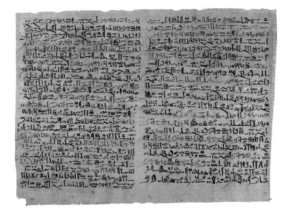

ABOVE: First translated in 1930, the Edwin Smith Papyrus challenged accepted views of the history of medicine.

Hippocratic Corpus

Hippocrates (ca. 460–370 BCE) played a vital role in establishing the idea of medicine as a profession and in refuting that disease was a punishment from the gods. Born on the sunny island of Kos in Greece in around 460 BCE, he learned medicine from his father and developed a substantial following of students throughout his lifetime. A collection of medical texts from the time carries his name, the Hippocratic Corpus, and although he may not actually have written them, he led the debate on their contents. The papers show an understanding of the tricuspid valve of the heart and a rudimentary appreciation of the musculoskeletal system.

A Ban on Human Dissection

In fairness to the ancient anatomists, progress was limited by a ban on human dissection. Aristotle (384–322 BCE) had worked on animal dissection, but it was the brief respite in this ban in the fourth century BCE that allowed for greater discovery. Two Greek physicians working in Alexandria, Egypt, worked fervently while the ban was lifted, identifying the ventricles of the brain and even establishing the difference between motor and sensory nerves. Their names were Herophilus and Erasistratus, but much of their work was lost when the library of Alexandria was destroyed in 391 CE A further eighteen hundred years were to pass before human dissection for anatomical study became legal again.

In the meantime, Roman physician Claudius Galenus (ca. 129–200 CE) worked on anatomy by dissecting macaque monkeys and pigs. Several of his observations (such as how the circulation system worked) remained uncontested for over a thousand years. His name still lives on inside us all: The word Galen describes not one, but two, veins that course through our skulls—the deep cerebral vein and the great cerebral vein.

> **FACT**
> In complete contradiction to the work of Galen, Syrian polymath Ibn al-Nafis (1213–1288) may have discovered that blood moved from the right to left side of the heart as early as the thirteenth century.

Art and Anatomy Side by Side: The Renaissance

Michelangelo's *David* (1504) and its vivid anatomical depiction poignantly reflect how art had overtaken science in the study of anatomy by the early sixteenth century. Belgian researcher Andreas Vesalius had revived dissection in Padua, but it was the work of the Renaissance artists that revolutionized our knowledge of the subject. They undertook painstaking studies of human cadavers and translated them into a form that the public could see. The availability of paper and movable type allowed that knowledge to spread as never before.

A Scientific Mind *No one symbolized the fusion between art and science more than Leonardo da Vinci. Born in the Tuscan hill town of Vinci within the jurisdiction of the powerful—and forward-thinking—Medici family, Leonardo had an inauspicious start to life. The son of an unmarried mother, he studied Latin, geometry, and mathematics on an informal basis before earning an apprenticeship under the Florentine painter Verrocchio at the age of fourteen.*

From there, he earned fame during his lifetime with

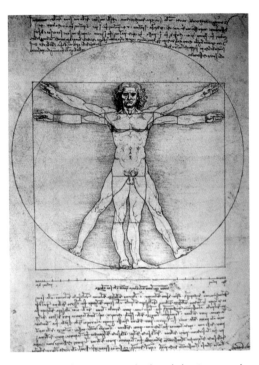

ABOVE: This iconic ink sketch by Leonardo da Vinci is known as the *Vitruvian Man*. It represents the idea of the correlation of human proportions with geometry.

his paintbrush, producing some of art's greatest works such as the Mona Lisa *and* The Last Supper. *Yet his drawings reveal a fiercely scientific mind as well. Sketches of flying machines, adding machines, and solar-powered batteries were found alongside his theories on plate tectonics. He also produced legendary anatomical drawings, such as that of the* Vitruvian Man.

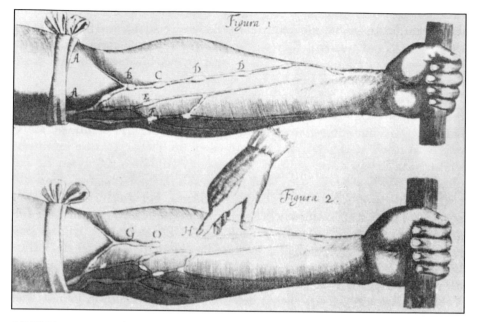

ABOVE: Harvey's classic experiment used only a tourniquet and gentle pressure to demonstrate the function of valves in maintaining unidirectional flow in veins.

Moving Anatomy: The Heart as a Pump

It is hard to believe now, but humans didn't realize that blood flowed around the body until long after Columbus had "discovered" the Americas. It was William Harvey (1578–1657), personal physician to the king of England, who is widely credited with demonstrating this fundamental shift in thinking. He had studied in Cambridge and Padua but it was his access to the Royal Courts—and frequent demonstrations of his work by using tourniquets in front of assembled courtiers—that advanced the acceptance of his theory. By allowing a tourniquet to interrupt the blood flow, he used the surface anatomy of veins to demonstrate the existence—and function—of the valves in them

Anatomy Beyond the Naked Eye

Arguably, the biggest shift in anatomy came with the invention of the microscope and the refinement of its use in the seventeenth century. For the first time in history, researchers could see small structures, such as capillary beds, and could observe bacteria and malarial parasites swimming in the blood. Today, electron microscopes (which use a beam of electrons rather than light) can magnify up to ten million times (as opposed to the two thousand magnification limit of a standard light microscope).

Radiology *Other developments in the twentieth century came from the emerging specialty of radiology: the clinical use of imaging techniques. Plain X-rays evolved into computerized tomography (CT scans), which showed the anatomy of the body slice by slice. Magnetic resonance imaging (MRI) used strong magnetic fields and radiowaves to show increased penetration of the soft tissues of the body.*

Positron emission tomography (PET) scans use nuclear medicine to visualize anatomical structures as they are working functionally. By administering tracers, it is possible to see exactly where a substance is being used through the detection of gamma-ray emissions. The body uses a substance called fludeoxyglucose, for example, in a similar way to regular glucose, allowing PET scans to visualize glucose metabolism in real time. The technique can be used clinically (in detecting cancer) as well as in an academic setting (to identify which parts of the brain are "active" during a particular task, and which are "inactive").

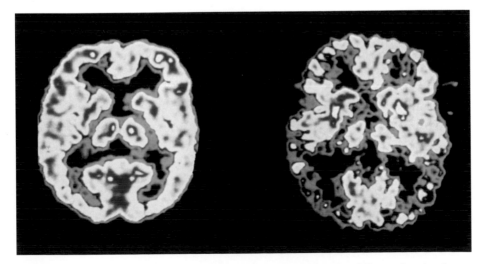

ABOVE: A PET Scan of the brain. Different colors reflect the different levels of cellular activity in the brain over time and during different circumstances.

> ✳ **FACT**
> In ancient Greece, leading athletes ate raw animals' testicles in order to enhance sporting performance. Today, sports stars have moved on to synthetic oxygen carriers like perflurocarbons (PFCs) in order to artificially enhance their performance.

The Rise of Sports Science and Medicine

In addition to the study of normal physiology (how the body works) and anatomy (how it is structured), humans have generally focused on the treatment and prevention of disease. Increasing fitness and performance as a goal of its own has had a more sporadic history. However, the foundation of the American College of Sports Medicine in 1954—to support the work of the new medical specialty—shows just how far attitudes and perceptions have changed with regard to how we look at anatomy.

Fashions in Anatomy

We share the same anatomy with all other humans across space and time, yet not all cultures share the same views on what looks good. From binding the feet of baby girls in China to using weights to elongate foreheads in Peru, fashion has prompted humans to try to change human anatomy in numerous ways. Today's trends include dieting to size zero, surgically chasing "high cheekbones," and injecting fillers to plump up sagging knees. Who knows what the future anatomical fashions will be?

2

FLUID
HIGHWAYS

Understanding Blood

Hematology involves the study of blood, the bodily fluid that has mesmerized humanity more than any other throughout history. Blood contains red blood cells (erythrocytes) that transport oxygen, white blood cells (leucocytes, which are subdivided into many different types), platelets, antibodies, and more. All of these constituents—along with hormones, electrolytes, cholesterol, and carbon dioxide—flow through our arteries and veins, either dissolved or suspended in a fluid called plasma.

The Hemoglobin Puzzle

Red blood cells get their color from hemoglobin, a red, oxygen-carrying protein. Max Perutz discovered the molecular structure of hemoglobin in the 1950s, marking a breakthrough in the field of molecular biology. Seeing the "shape" of hemoglobin enabled Perutz to discover that each hemoglobin molecule binds four oxygen molecules. Not all oxygen is bound equally, however.

Once one oxygen molecule has bound, hemoglobin begins to change shape, making it easier for more oxygen to bind. The same is true in reverse: Once one oxygen molecule is released, the rest follow easily. Since the prime job of hemoglobin (Hb in scientific shorthand) is to transport oxygen from an area of relatively high concentration (the lungs) to an area of low concentration (the capillary beds), such properties are valuable.

FACT

How much blood do we have? The traditional answer to this question is eight pints (five liters). In reality, of course, how much blood you have depends on your height, weight, and frame. Olympic oarsman Steve Redgrave will have rather more blood than Hollywood actor Angelina Jolie.

Table of Blood Constituents

Component	Structure & Function
Red blood cells (Erythrocytes)	Transport oxygen bound to hemoglobin. They have a lifespan of around 120 days.
Platelets	Megakaryocyte cell fragments essential for clotting. They have a lifespan of around five to nine days.
White blood cells—Neutrophils	First line of defense against invading microorganisms.
White blood cells—Lymphocytes (B Cells, T Cells, and Natural Killer Cells)	More advanced part of the immune system. Help to coordinate immune memory.
White blood cells—Eosinophils	Release histamine to fight parasites. All white blood cells have a lifespan of around a few hours to a few days.
Albumin	Transports hormones, ions, drugs, and waste. Maintains the colloid pressure of the blood
Lipoproteins	Bind and transport cholesterol
Clotting factors	Includes Factor VIII. Responsible for activating clotting.
Immunoglobulins/Antibodies	Bind to recognized pathogens as part of the immune response
Dissolved gases—oxygen and carbon dioxide	Substrate and waste product of respiration
Hormones	Adrenaline, cortisol, thyroxine, and more. Induce complex metabolic changes throughout the body.
Ions	$Na+$, $K+$, Ca_2+, HCO_3-, Mg_2+, and more. Crucial to neuromuscular function and transport across cell membranes.
Glucose	Also known as "blood sugar." Provides energy to cells throughout the body.
Fibrinogen	A glycoprotein that becomes fibrin when activated to help form part of a blood clot.

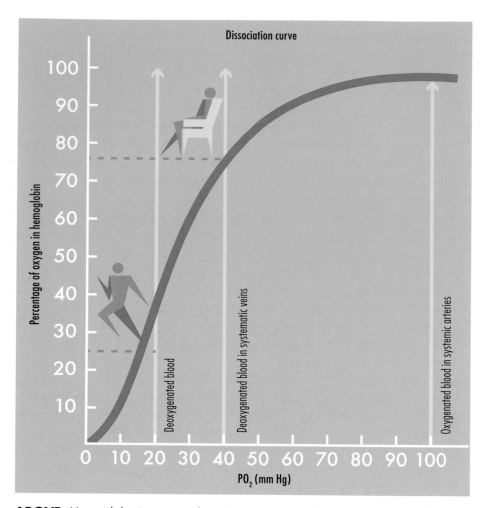

ABOVE: Hemoglobin's oxygen-dissociation curve in chart form. It is useful for demonstrating how the blood carries and releases oxygen.

The Bohr Effect *The "tipping point" for oxygen binding or release can be altered by other chemicals in the body. High levels of carbon dioxide or hydrogen ions make hemoglobin more likely to release oxygen, while low levels prompt hemoglobin to keep hold of it. Thus, as active cells use up oxygen and produce more carbon dioxide, the hemoglobin curve shifts to the right and more oxygen is delivered to the cells. Anesthetists can manipulate these factors during surgery to ensure an adequate level of oxygen exchange at a tissue level. Max Perutz earned himself a Nobel Prize for his work.*

Blood Pressure

When people talk about blood pressure, they are usually talking about arterial blood pressure. It is expressed as two values: a systolic number representing the contraction of the heart and a lower, diastolic number, which represents the relaxation of the heart. Blood pressure exists on a continuous scale but, for healthy adults, normal blood pressure is approximately 110/70 mm Hg. Values reach 20–40 mm Hg in the capillaries and hover just above zero in the venous system.

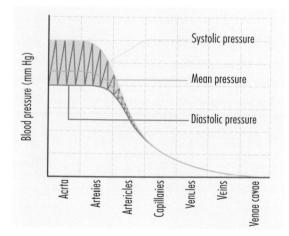

LEFT: A chart demonstrating the average systolic and diastolic pressure for different regions of the circulatory system.

Hemorrhage and the Clotting Cascade

Coagulation (thrombogenesis) is the process of forming a blood clot. When bleeding occurs, injured cells lining the blood vessels (the endothelium) trigger a build up of platelets and fibrin strands through the chemical factors of what is called the clotting cascade. They form a clot (thrombus) and control the hemorrhage.

Athletes are frequently removed from competitive matches to receive treatment for small bleeds sustained during a game. Sometimes pressure and time are enough for a primary clot to form and an athlete can return. In some cases, however, wounds need to be covered or sutured. Such precautions are taken because of the potential risk of blood-borne diseases such as HIV, Hepatitis B, and Hepatitis C.

Blood Transfusions

There are many reasons for needing a blood transfusion. Bleeding is the obvious one, although there are others, usually when blood production (hematopoiesis) is impaired in some way. Whole blood is rarely used these days, because its separate components (red cells, platelets, fresh frozen plasma, and so on) offer more targeted therapy with fewer side effects. Blood transfusions carry risks, of course, through the transmission of disease—which is rare—or through a transfusion reaction (also rare).

Blood Groups *Blood, and some blood products, need to be matched between the donor and the recipient. We all carry antigens on the walls of our cells—various proteins, glycoproteins, glycolipids, and so on— that send signals to our immune system to help it differentiate between our own cells and those of an invading organism. The problem arises when antigens from another person are mistaken as dangerous and the immune system is activated. To prevent blood transfusions from killing the people they are supposed to help, various blood group classifications have been devised, the most important one being the ABO system.*

	Group A	Group B	Group AB	Group O
Red blood cell type	A	B	AB	O
Antibodies in plasma	Anti-B	Anti-A	None	Anti-A and Anti-B
Antigens in red blood cell	A antigen	B antigen	A and B antigen	None

ABOVE: In the ABO system, classification is determined by the antibodies present in the plasma and the antigens present in the red blood cells.

> **FACT**
> Excess red cells in the blood make it less fluid and more prone to clotting. Clots interrupt blood flow and, depending on where they form, can induce strokes, heart attacks, limb injuries, and gut damage.

The Universal Donor *"O Neg" is frequently referred to as the universal donor blood type. It lacks A, B, and Rhesus antigens on its red cells and can be given to anyone without triggering a reaction based on those (the most common) antigens. However, other antigen–antibody reactions exist and, under ideal situations, a full crossmatch is usually preferred. A crossmatch is a laboratory simulation whereby the donor's red cells and the recipient's plasma are matched together to look for adverse reactions. In life-threatening emergencies where there is no time for this, O Neg blood remains the safest to give.*

Blood Doping in Sports

Blood doping involves using a blood transfusion to increase artificially the red cell count—and, therefore, oxygen carrying capacity—of the blood. It has been in practice for decades. Its use by elite endurance athletes peaked in the 1970s and then tailed off as synthetic erythropoietin (EPO), which stimulates red cell production, became available. Later, as EPO-detecting tests improved, blood transfusions became popular again.

Transfusions can be either from someone else (homologous) or from oneself to oneself (autologous), with enough of a gap in between to make the procedure worthwhile. In hospitals, autologous transfusions are performed ahead of elective surgery that has a high risk of hemorrhage. Outside hospitals, they are performed ahead of a main race or tournament. Autologous transfusions are safer in either case and, when it comes to doping, they are harder to detect. However, these transfusions are less "effective" for athletes because of the time lost to training surrounding the blood donation phase.

The Blood–Brain Barrier

Contrary to thousands of years of poetry, it is the brain, and not the heart, that is sensitive to insults from the outside world. Cerebral tissue requires a strictly controlled environment, and yet the level of chemicals within the blood changes from one minute to the next. The solution to this problem is the blood–brain barrier.

Within the brain, the cells that line the blood vessels (the endothelium) and their supporting cells (astrocytes) provide both a physical and metabolic barrier. "Tight junctions" between endothelial cells limit the passage of larger molecules and cells, while carefully calibrated transport mechanisms within the cells themselves allow the selective passage of essential blood components, such as glucose, across the cell membrane.

Cerebrospinal Fluid *The fluid that sits around the brain and spinal cord is called cerebrospinal fluid (CSF). Produced by the choroid plexus in the ventricles of the brain, its role is to cushion the central nervous system. The total volume at any one time is around 3½–4½ fluid ounces (100–160 milliliters) but as the fluid is constantly being reabsorbed, the body produces around one pint (500 milliliters) per day.*

Lymph

Everyone knows about veins and arteries, but for some unfortunate reason, lymph often gets overlooked. Lymph is the "leftover" fluid that forms in the interstitial tissue of capillary beds once fluid and substance exchange has taken place.

When oxygenated arterial blood reaches the capillaries, proteins, cells, gases, substrates, and more ooze out into the interstitial tissue. At the same time, waste products ooze back into the blood, along with the majority of the fluid that first oozed out. That deoxygenated blood flows into the venous system and back to the heart.

However, around six pints (three liters) of interstitial fluid per day isn't reabsorbed in the capillaries. Instead, it becomes lymph and it flows back toward the heart through the low-pressure lymphatic vessels. In particular, lipid-rich (fat-rich) fluid absorbed from the small intestine enters the lymphatic system instead of the blood, bypassing the first pass metabolism of the liver.

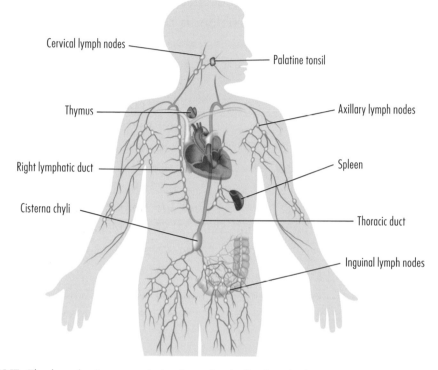

ABOVE: The lymphatic system helps keep body fluids in balance. It also helps protect the body against harmful bacteria and viruses.

Gland Trouble *The lymphatic system ensures that lymph passes through lymph nodes en route, providing an excellent chance for specialized white blood cells (lymphocytes) to notice external threats and mount an immune response. The activation of these lymph nodes is why our glands can feel tender and swollen during an infection. Lymph nodes are also able to detect cancerous cells that have spread from an original tumor and destroy them. Sadly, this isn't always possible, and in such cases the lymphatic system serves as a conduit for the cancerous tissue to spread further throughout the body in a process called metastasis.*

Who Needs a Spleen?

Plenty of people know that a human can live without his or her spleen, but what does it actually do? The spleen is a domed, jellyfish-shaped organ that sits tucked behind the ninth, tenth, and eleventh ribs on the left-hand side of the abdomen. It is the largest collection of lymphoid tissue in the body and has several hematological functions. Its many sinuses and generous blood flow allow it to function as a reservoir of blood and place it in an ideal situation to "filter" the circulating volume. Thus, as red blood cells reach the end of their 120-day cycle, the spleen recycles them, breaking down the hemoglobin into its "hem" and "globin" parts, and converting them into bilirubin and amino acids respectively.

The white pulp of the spleen consists of lymphoid nodules, which play an important part in leading the immune response against certain bacteria.

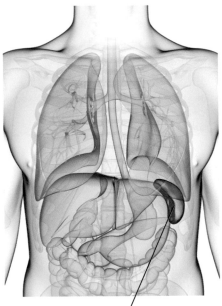

Spleen

LEFT: The spleen is about the size and shape of a clenched fist.

Ruptured Spleen *Although reasonably well protected by the ribcage, a healthy spleen can still be at risk, particularly in automobile accidents or when cycling—the latter, because the abdomen is likely to strike the handlebars on the falling trajectory. In fact, blunt trauma from rugby, soccer, snowboarding (knees to abdomen during a fall), hockey, football, and fighting in the street can all damage the spleen. If the injury is small, bleeding can sometimes be contained within the spleen's capsule. Because of the spleen's rich blood flow, however, splenic injury can be life threatening and surgeons frequently need to remove the organ altogether if they cannot control the bleeding.*

The Heart

Despite our longing for it in terms of love, courage, and other poetic fancies, the heart in the human body functions principally as a mechanical pump. It has two "pump circuits" that work together. The right side of the heart (right atrium and right ventricle) pumps deoxygenated blood from the body to the lungs via the pulmonary artery. The left side of the heart (left atrium and left ventricle) pumps oxygenated blood from the lungs to the rest of the body via the aorta. Rinse and repeat. And repeat. And repeat.

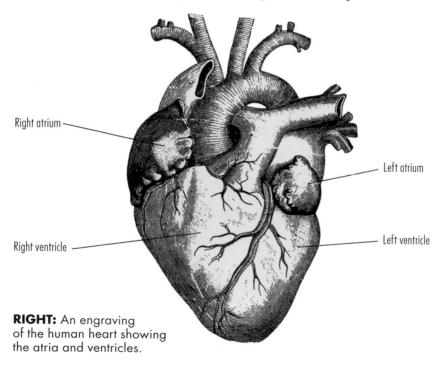

Right atrium

Left atrium

Right ventricle

Left ventricle

RIGHT: An engraving of the human heart showing the atria and ventricles.

FACT

Heart Health. A healthy heart beats around 100,000 times a day. It pumps some 15,850 pints (7,500 liters) of blood around the body through an incredible 60,000 miles (96,500 kilometers) of blood vessels.

Pulse Control

The heart has a natural pacemaker: the sinoatrial node. Situated in the right atrium, the sinoatrial node sends an electrical signal across the atria of the heart. The electrical charge then gathers at the atrioventricular node, allowing for a refractory delay while the atria contract and relax, after which the electrical charge spreads further into the ventricles. The signal travels along the Bundle of His to the Purkinje fibers, which spread the charge throughout the ventricles. Without these specialized conducting systems, the electrical charge could "paralyze" the heart.

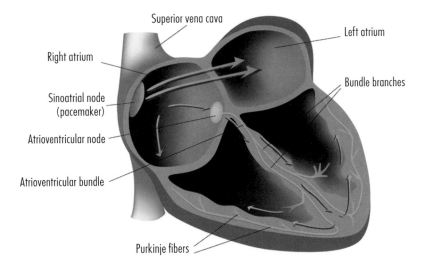

ABOVE: A cutaway diagram to show the electrical pathways of the heart. The impulse for the heartbeat begins in the sinoatrial node.

Fluid Dynamics

The human body has substantially more blood vessels than it has blood to flow through them. By constricting or relaxing the muscles in arteries and arterioles—and to a lesser extent in veins—we can selectively redirect our blood to where we need it the most. We can see this in action when we look at our own skin during changes in temperature. When we are hot, our blood vessels relax (vasodilate), allowing more blood to flow through our skin to help us lose heat. When we are cold, we vasoconstrict to conserve heat.

Cardiac Output

This is the volume of blood pumped out by the heart in a single minute. At rest, it is approximately eight pints (five liters) per minute, but this increases during exercise and in response to certain disease states.

Cardiac Output (Q) = SV × HR

Where SV is stroke volume (the volume of blood pumped by the ventricle in a single beat) and HR is heart rate. Stroke volume is influenced by the amount of blood returned to the heart just before each heartbeat. Emotions such as fear, drugs such as caffeine or cocaine, and the effects of fever can increase heart rate.

Heart rate is easy to measure indirectly by feeling a pulse, while stroke volume is difficult to measure in a noninvasive way. Most techniques to approximate stroke volume rely on the Fick principle, which uses oxygen consumption as an approximation. By sampling the oxygen content of venous blood and arterial blood, and by recording a person's oxygen consumption per minute, we can calculate cardiac output by using the following formula:

$Q = (VO_2/(C_A - C_V)) \star 100$

Where VO_2 is oxygen consumption, C_A is the oxygen content of arterial blood, and C_V is the oxygen content of venous blood. However, even these samples are difficult to obtain outside a laboratory or intensive-care setting.

Cardiologists use ultrasounds of the heart (echocardiography) to visualize blood flow and calculate CO and SV. In more everyday clinical practice, physicians rely on a combination of pulse and blood pressure to assess the health of the circulatory system.

> ✳ **FACT**
> Many physically fit young men have a pulse of below fifty beats per minute at rest. This cardiac output would be considered dangerously low under similar circumstances in other adults.

Heart Attacks and Cardiac Arrest

A "heart attack" refers to myocardial infarction (MI), where an insufficient blood supply leads to the death of myocardial tissue. Cardiac arrest means that the heart has stopped beating. Myocardial infarctions are one of the commonest causes of cardiac arrest in adults, but they are not the only cause. Furthermore, not all myocardial infarctions lead to cardiac arrest—it depends on which part of the heart is damaged. There are instances in which cardiac arrest can cause a myocardial infarction. For example, if an irregular heartbeat (arrhythmia) led to the arrest, the cardiac arrest itself would limit blood flow to the heart, which could cause a myocardial infarction during the resuscitation period.

Sudden Cardiac Death

Sudden cardiac death is defined as an event that is nontraumatic, nonviolent, unexpected, and resulting from sudden cardiac arrest within six hours of previously witnessed normal health. Sometimes, apparently healthy young people simply drop down dead. The sudden cardiac arrest of soccer player Fabrice Muamba during a game highlighted the importance of effective cardiopulmonary resuscitation (CPR) and postresuscitation care. It also fueled the discussion about screening for the underlying conditions that may cause these tragedies.

3

THE MUSCULO-SKELETAL SYSTEM

Living Bones

Bones have a somewhat dry and dusty image that they simply don't deserve. Once we die, bones do resemble the brittle, white, stick-like motifs that decorate Halloween costumes. But in living human beings, bones are extremely dynamic, flexible, and complex physiological and anatomical structures.

Our bones remodel themselves constantly throughout life so that each bone in the body gets replaced every ten years or so. As well as growing steadily throughout childhood, bones also become tougher and stronger as a result of high-impact exercise (a process known as hypertrophy). Bones are also prone to becoming weaker through inactivity (atrophy). In both of these respects bones are similar to muscles.

Bones hurt when they are injured and bleed when they break. They also play a vital role in maintaining the body's levels of calcium, magnesium, and phosphate salts, and their bone marrow produces blood cells (white and red) and platelets (a process called hematopoiesis).

The Skeleton

For anatomical study, the human skeleton is divided into two parts: the axial skeleton (skull, vertebrae, ribs, and sternum) and the appendicular skeleton (limbs and pelvis).

FACT
Round, pebble-like sesamoid bones are so-called because their shape reminded ancient anatomists of sesame seeds. They are usually found when a tendon passes over a joint. Their function is to protect the tendon from wear and to change the angle of traction during movement. The largest and best-known sesamoid bone is the patella—commonly called the knee cap.

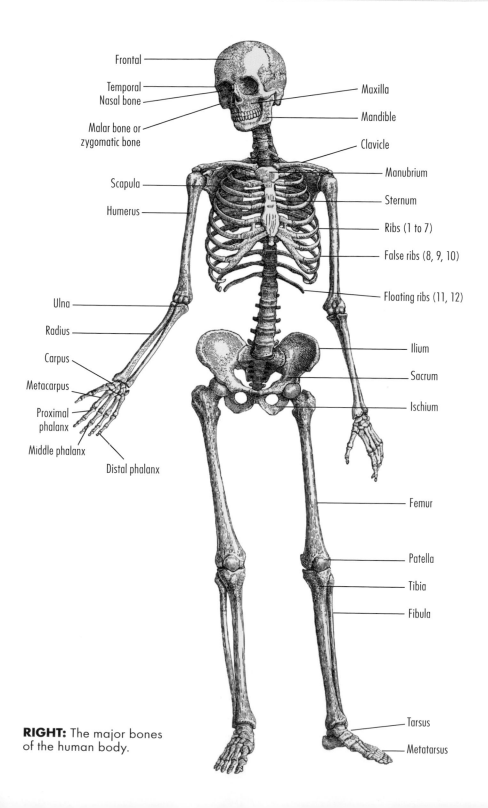

Frontal

Temporal
Nasal bone

Malar bone or
zygomatic bone

Scapula

Humerus

Ulna

Radius

Carpus

Metacarpus

Proximal
phalanx

Middle phalanx

Distal phalanx

Maxilla

Mandible

Clavicle

Manubrium

Sternum

Ribs (1 to 7)

False ribs (8, 9, 10)

Floating ribs (11, 12)

Ilium

Sacrum

Ischium

Femur

Patella

Tibia

Fibula

Tarsus

Metatarsus

RIGHT: The major bones
of the human body.

How Many Bones Are There in the Human Skeleton?

The answer to this question should be easy, but differences between individuals makes it difficult to pinpoint. Some people have extra ribs, while others grow additional bones, particularly in sites of previous injury. With all of the caveats in place, the conventional answer is 205.

The Bones in the Body

Bone Group	Individual Bones
Cranial Bones	Frontal, Parietal (x2), Temporal (x2), Occipital, Sphenoid
Facial Bones	Mandible, Maxilla (x2), Palatine (x2), Zygomatic (x2), Nasal (x2), Lacrimal (x2), Inferior nasal concha (x2), Vomer
Middle Ears	Malleus (x2), Incus (x2), Stapes (x2)
Throat	Hyoid
Shoulder Girdles	Scapula (x2), Clavicle (x2)
Thorax	Sternum (includes body, manubrium, and xiphoid process), Ribs (2 x12)
Vertebral Column	Cervical vertebrae (x7), Thoracic vertebrae (x12), Lumbar vertebrae (x5)
Arms	Humerus (x2), Radius (x2), Ulna (x2)
Wrists	Scaphoid (x2), Lunate (x2), Triquetrum (x2), Pisiform (x2), Hamate (x2), Capitate (x2), Trapezium (x2), Trapezoid (x2)
Hands	Metacarpals (5 x2), Proximal phalanges (5 x2), Intermediate phalanges (5 x2), Distal phalanges (5 x2)
Pelvis	Sacrum, Coccyx, Ilium (x2), Ischium (x2), Pubis (x2)
Legs	Femur (x2), Patella (x2), Tibia (x2), Fibula (x2)
Ankle and Foot	Calcaneum (x2), Talus (x2), Navicular bone (x2), Medial cuneiform (x2), Intermediate cuneiform (x2), Lateral cuneiform (x2), Cuboid (x2), Metatarsals (5 x2)
Toes	Proximal phalanges (5 x2), Intermediate phalanges (5 x2), Distal phalanges (5 x2)

Our Complex Skull

The human skull is a jigsaw of several different bones, connected by immobile sutures or seams. The jaw (mandible) is the exception to this, and can take bites via movement through the temporomandibular joint. The solid, fixed nature of the skull protects the brain from external injuries. That same fixed nature can also quickly lead to problems, however. It only takes a small hemorrhage, for example, to cause significant damage, as the space reserved for cerebral tissue is replaced by blood.

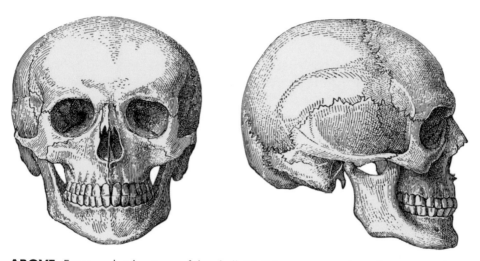

ABOVE: Front and side views of the skull. Visible sutures on the side view are the cranial (across the top), squamosal (above the ear), and lambdoid (to the rear).

At birth, the skull has much greater flexibility. Membranes replace bone in some parts known as fontanelles. The most significant of these are the posterior and anterior fontanelles, which close by twelve and eighteen months respectively. Before then, it is possible to feel these soft spots on a baby's head.

The reason for our skulls not being fully fused at birth is to ease passage along the birth canal. It takes years for the skull's sutures to fuse permanently.

Bone Marrow

Bone marrow is a spongy tissue that can be found inside some of the bones of the skeleton (in the arms and legs, for example). It is red if it principally contains cells that produce blood cells and platelets (hematopoietic tissue) or yellow if it principally contains fat. As we grow older, much of our active red bone marrow is replaced with the yellow, fatty type.

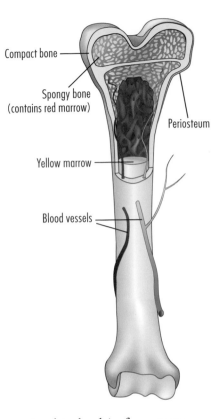

Compact bone

Spongy bone
(contains red marrow)

Periosteum

Yellow marrow

Blood vessels

RIGHT: The anatomy of a living bone. The cross-section at the top reveals how bone marrow is arranged within a long bone.

How Bones Heal *Once broken, bones tend to heal in four stages. When the break occurs, there is significant bleeding into nearby tissue.*

1. *Clotting begins and a hematoma forms. Cells called fibroblasts move into the hematoma and begin laying down granulation tissue to form a soft callus.*

2. *After a few weeks, the soft callus is stable enough for osteoblast cells to produce new bone.*

3. *Over the next six to twelve weeks, calcium and phosphate minerals are incorporated to form a hard callus. At this point in the process, plaster casts are usually removed and a period of physical therapy begins.*

4. *The final stage involves bone remodeling, when excess bone is naturally trimmed back and the smoother contours of the original bone are returned. This final stage is a process that can last up to several years.*

Why Do We Use Plaster Casts? *Immobility is crucial for bone healing—up to a point. At first, blood needs to clot to prevent further bleeding and to allow fibroblasts to move in. The soft callus is also vulnerable to disruption, so immobility can be helpful then. However, bones require some kind of weight bearing to heal in the correct configuration, and too much immobility can lead to stiffness and eventual loss of function. Therefore, fracture management usually focuses on the balance between movement and immobility during the healing process of a broken or fractured bone. Metalwork is sometimes used when a plaster is not appropriate—either because the break is too unstable or because the anatomy of the injured part does not allow for a plaster. (No one wants a skull plaster, after all.)*

- *Stable fractures of the digits can be treated by binding a digit to its neighbor. This maintains the position of the broken fragments while preventing spiral movements from pulling them apart.*
- *Rib and clavicle fractures are usually left to heal without any immobilization. (Although painful, it is still better to be able to move enough to breathe.)*

FACT

Bones can break as a result of repeated use with insufficient rest in between. These breaks are known as stress fractures and are, not surprisingly, found in military recruits, amateur marathon runners, and professional athletes across a range of sports—particularly in the metatarsals of the feet and the tibia of the lower leg.

The Spine

The vertebrae of the neck not only bear the weight of the head, but they also allow it to move in order to maximize the senses of sight, smell, and hearing housed in the head. The first cervical vertebra (the atlas or C1) supports the head and pivots around the odontoid peg of the second vertebra (the axis or C2.)

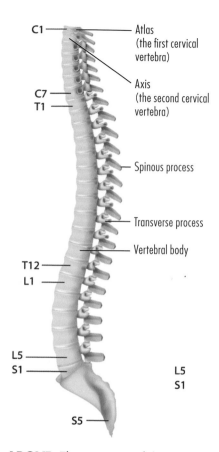

Slipped Disks

Intervertebral disks are cartilaginous structures that sit between each vertebra (except between the atlas and axis of C1 and C2). They're made of a fibrocartilaginous outer donut ring called the annulus fibrosus, which surrounds a jelly-like

ABOVE: The anatomy of the human spine.

central nucleus pulposus. Together, they provide a kind of shock absorption for the spine, dehydrating slowly over the course of the day and rehydrating during sleep, when the body lies horizontal. Disks don't actually "slip," but the central nucleus pulposus can herniate through its containing annulus fibrosus. This causes pain (and sometimes nerve damage) if the extruded contents press on the nerve roots as they exit the spine.

Understanding Spinal Injuries

As neurons exit the spinal cord, they recombine to create peripheral nerves. These "nerve roots" are labeled so that physicians and anatomists can keep track: C for cervical, T for thoracic, L for lumbar, and S for sacral, each with a number to demonstrate the sequence of the vertebrae in the chain. Spinal injuries are, therefore, often described by the "level" at which the cord is affected: For example, T10 injuries will cause a loss of sensation at the umbilicus and below, together with a loss of motor function for muscles supplied by nerve roots from T10 and below.

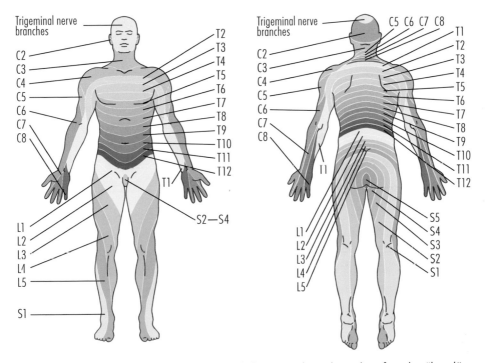

ABOVE: Dermatomes of the body—each letter and number identifies the "level" at which a nerve root leaves the spinal cord.

"C3, 4, 5 Keeps the Diaphragm Alive"

Before the age of ventilators, the key factor affecting survival after a spinal injury was whether or not the supply to the phrenic nerve was still intact. The phrenic nerve supplies the diaphragm—the most important muscle involved in breathing and also the one with the "highest" nerve supply. C3, 4, and 5 combine to form the phrenic nerve and so spinal injuries at C3 or above are likely to be fatal without immediate medical intervention.

Muscles

Muscles are the action heroes of our anatomy and physiology, or so we believe. They include the quads and the biceps, the pecs, and the hamstrings. They allow us to run, jump, swim, fight, and sashay into the kitchen for a cold drink. But they also bring our poetry to life, caress our lovers, and reach out a hand to wipe away our tears. No matter what we think, all we can do is move. Whether it's in the blink of an eye or the running of a marathon.

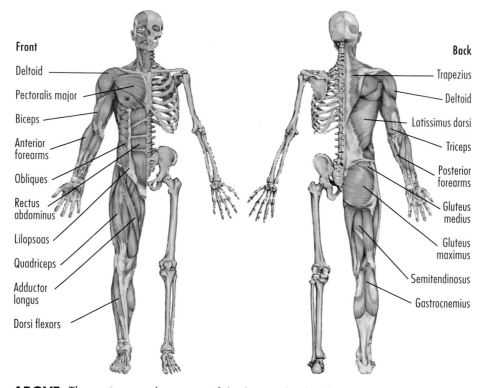

Front

- Deltoid
- Pectoralis major
- Biceps
- Anterior forearms
- Obliques
- Rectus abdominus
- Lilopsoas
- Quadriceps
- Adductor longus
- Dorsi flexors

Back

- Trapezius
- Deltoid
- Latissimus dorsi
- Triceps
- Posterior forearms
- Gluteus medius
- Gluteus maximus
- Semitendinosus
- Gastrocnemius

ABOVE: The major muscle groups of the human body—front and back. They include the deltoids, the obliques, and the gluteus muscles.

Smooth, Striated, or Cardiac?

Not all muscles are created equal. At a cellular level, muscle cells (myocytes) look different, depending on the way they work and the different functions they perform.

Smooth Muscle *Smooth muscle is largely involuntary. It is responsible for the movement that propels food through the digestive system (peristalsis), uterine contractions during labor, constricting blood vessels, squeezing bile ducts, and much, much more.*

Striated Muscle *Striated muscle appears stripy under the microscope, reflecting the arrangement of actin and myosin filaments, which allow coordinated, voluntary contraction of the muscle when activated by an electrical charge. The myosin slides across the actin filaments using a ratchet mechanism to shorten the distance between the fibers. The body must then spend energy undoing these bonds to return the muscles to their relaxed state. The electrical charge necessary for muscle contraction comes about via the effects of neurotransmitters released by nerve endings on the ion channels of the myocyte itself.*

Since this voluntary muscle is usually attached via tendons to the skeleton, it also goes by the name of skeletal muscle. Fast-twitch fibers provide brief but intense energy, whereas slow-twitch fibers allow for slower, sustained contractions.

Cardiac Muscle *Cardiac muscle has its own identity entirely. It is involuntary but also striated. Its actin and myosin filaments are branched rather than linear and are designed for fast, synchronized contraction. This muscle type is found only in the heart.*

The Science of Bodybuilding

For a long while, it was thought that muscle was either "fast" or "slow," based on the speed of its contraction and then relaxation. When scientists looked at bird muscle, "fast" muscle appeared white and "slow" red, as a reflection of the differing amounts of myoglobin (muscle's answer to hemoglobin—an oxygen-binding molecule) and the volumes of their capillary networks. The idea was also put forward that exercise could change one type of muscle to the other. Now things appear a little more complicated.

Regardless of the name, though, there is an overall trade-off between speed and fatigability within our muscle fibers. And to some extent, those features can be changed. Regular endurance training does increase the oxidative capacity of all muscle types. We see an increase in capillary density as well as more mitochondria (the powerhouse of the cell) and aerobic enzymes within each fiber.

FACT

The smallest muscle in the body is stapedius, which dampens excess vibration in the middle ear. It measures just 0.04 inch (1 mm) in length.

High Load, Low Repetition *High-intensity resistance training causes hypertrophy of muscle fibers by increasing the volume of contractile proteins within the muscle fibers themselves. This increases strength as well as building bulk—and is responsible for the visible changes we see in bodybuilding. The reverse also occurs. Without regular use, our body questions why it puts all that effort into making contractile proteins, enzymes, and the like, if we're not going to use them. So it scales back. Oxidative capacity reduces. Muscle bulk fades away.*

The Neck—A Crucial Part of the Musculoskeletal Highway

For a small space, the neck has a lot going on. It contains the larynx and trachea, essential for talking, singing, and breathing. It contains the esophagus for eating, the thyroid gland for controlling metabolism, and that's not all. Vessel-wise there's the powerhouse carotid and vertebral arteries and the system of jugular veins. As well as lymph glands, the neck houses baroreceptors that detect changes in blood pressure and send signals back to the brainstem, as well as chemoreceptors sensitive to changes in blood pH. Since pH falls as carbon dioxide levels rise, and carbon dioxide is a waste product of metabolism, this information is vital in making us take another breath: more oxygen in, more carbon dioxide out.

The Internal Jugular Vein—A Window into the Heart

The state of the right atrium can give physicians valuable information as to how well (or not) the heart is working. While echocardiography and radioactive imaging provide more precise data, a quick glance from a trained eye can reveal plenty if you know where to look.

The superior vena cava (SVC) is one of the two great veins that empty into the right atrium, and there are only a few veins between the internal jugular vein and the SVC with no valves in between. When standing up, the internal jugular vein usually collapses, while, when lying down, it fills up. With someone sitting at an angle of forty-five degrees, the height of the column of blood and its waveform can give clues as to the functioning of the right side of the heart.

The Larynx

The larynx consists of three paired cartilages (the arytenoids, corniculates, and cuneiforms), three individual pieces of cartilage (thyroid, epiglottis, and cricoid), and the intrinsic muscles that bind the whole thing together like a finely articulated model ship. As well as protecting the entrance to the trachea, the larynx also houses the vocal cords—infoldings of mucous membranes that allow babies to scream, prima donnas to soar, and the rest of us to keep the social oil of conversation going through day to day pleasantries and chit chat. The larynx stretches and thins the cords to produce higher notes, and relaxes them for deeper tones. The thyroid cartilage at the front becomes more prominent during puberty for men, providing both a deeper voice and the visible "Adam's apple."

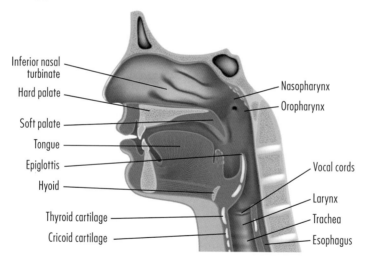

ABOVE: The anatomy of the larynx, showing both its location within the neck and its primary structures.

Above them all sits the epiglottis, a curved piece of cartilage designed to snap down shut the moment a foreign body heads its way. Anesthetists use the tip of the epiglottis as an important landmark when intubating patients (passing a tube directly into the trachea) to maintain a definitive airway (one protected from mucus, blood, or foreign bodies).

4

BRAIN
POWER

The Brain

In scientific terms, understanding the brain is the closest we may get to comprehending the soul. Our brains house our memories, our personalities, our dreams, and our ideas about identity. Yet alongside such lofty roles, the brain also controls when we eat, when we wash, and whether or not we remember to pick up the dry cleaning or to take out the garbage.

Brain Makeup

When looking at the anatomy of the brain—both structurally and functionally—it is as if we have three "evolutionary" brains. The cortex is the most adaptive and skilled part, responsible for speech, creativity, and decision-making. Then comes an intermediate system—called the limbic system—which governs our emotions and instinctive responses. At the most primitive, yet crucial, level is the brainstem. Sometimes referred to as the "vegetative center," it provides central control for breathing, appetite, and circulation.

Chain of Command *Each area of the brain follows a strict hierarchy of command, from the simple and primitive to the complex and civilized. Following a loud bang, for example, the auditory nerve feeds information to the lower hearing centers that are responsible for primitive responses, such as the startle reflex. But information also flows on to higher centers in the cortex, where the sound is examined further (is it speech, is it music, what does it mean?) and then compared to other sensory stimuli (how does the sound relate to what I can see?) and memory (have I heard this sound before?).*

Sharp Reflexes *Processing information in this way allows the primitive "fight or flight" reflexes to set in motion before the higher evaluative functions take place. The cortex reflects the finest analysis of sensory integration, learning, and skill. The cortex is rudimentary in reptiles and becomes more developed in mammals, reaching prominence in primates. Human beings have the most developed cortex of all.*

Loud Noises *People who are rendered "cortically deaf" following damage to the auditory cortex are not consciously aware of hearing and cannot follow speech through sound. Yet their startle reflex is still present and they will still jump in response to an unexpected loud noise—even though they cannot "hear" it.*

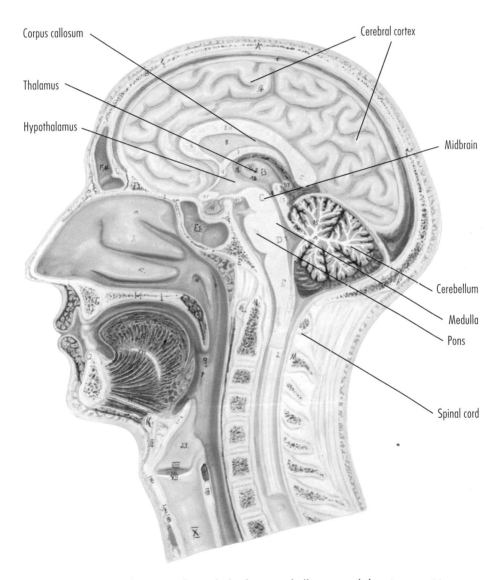

Corpus callosum

Cerebral cortex

Thalamus

Hypothalamus

Midbrain

Cerebellum

Medulla

Pons

Spinal cord

ABOVE: A sagittal section through the human skull to reveal the size, position, and composition of the brain within.

Mapping Out the Cerebral Cortex

Throughout history, humans have tried to map out the surface of the brain and attribute specific functions to each area. As neuroscience has progressed, while it has been slightly disappointing to discover just how difficult this is to do with any great accuracy, certain areas have become clear:

- *The back (occipital) part of the cerebral cortex deals with visual processing.*
- *An area found on the side deals with auditory processing.*
- *The first processing point for the sensation of touch (the primary somatosensory cortex) lives in the post-central ridge of the cortex.*
- *The primary motor cortex lies just in front on the back (posterior) portion of the frontal lobe.*

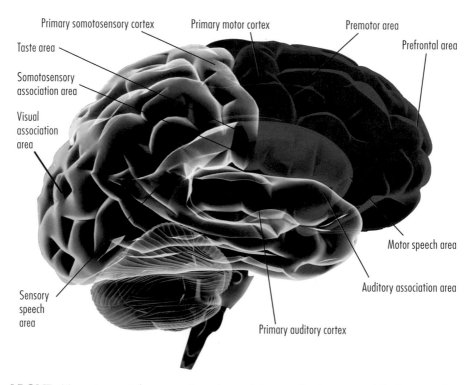

Primary somotosensory cortex   Primary motor cortex   Premotor area

Taste area   Prefrontal area

Somotosensory association area

Visual association area

Motor speech area

Sensory speech area   Auditory association area

Primary auditory cortex

ABOVE: Mapping out the many functions of the cerebral cortex. Which part of the brain does what, exactly?

The Basal Ganglia *The basal ganglia are a group of nuclei in the brain that deal with aspects of procedural memory and motor control. Their component parts are called the striatum (which itself consists of the caudate nucleus and putamen), the globus pallidus, the substantia nigra, the nucleus accumbens, and the subthalamic nucleus. The large striatum receives information from several sources but only sends information on to the rest of the basal ganglia.*

FACT

Nerve cells in the substantia nigra produce dopamine, a chemical that helps coordinate body movement. Degeneration of the substantia nigra results in a loss of these nerve cells, causing Parkinson's Disease, whereby people have difficulty initiating movement.

The Yips *The term "yips" refers to the sudden loss of fine motor skills in sportsmen and sportswomen, which occurs for no obvious reason. While it's often used as a golfing term, the yips can also make an unwanted appearance for cricket bowlers and baseball pitchers and even snooker and darts players. The cause is unclear, although it does seem to follow excessive use of a small group of muscles and is more common in athletes with long careers. One theory suggests that it results from uncontrolled firing in the motor cortex responsible for the affected area. The condition does appear to improve with rest.*

A Change of Personality *The most forward (anterior) part of the frontal lobe is called the pre-frontal cortex and, according to scientists, it is possibly the most highly developed part of the brain. It's the part that weighs up decisions and overrides the most basic instincts (to go home and go to bed, to react in anger, to burst into tears, to urinate on the spot, to cheat in an exam). It functions as both our social and moral compass.*

Much interest in the role of the pre-frontal cortex arose following the unfortunate accident of Phineas Gage. A U.S. construction worker, he sustained an injury during a rock blast that propelled an iron bar straight through his skull, piercing his left eye and damaging the frontal lobe of his brain, before exiting his skull. Although he survived, he was left with substantial behavioral and personality changes.

 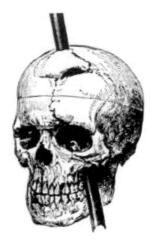

LEFT & ABOVE: Phineas Gage and a demonstration of the iron bar that penetrated his skull. His case provided an insight into how different parts of the brain work.

The Limbic System

The limbic system deals with emotions and stereotypical behavior, or as many of us prefer to call it, instinct. The anatomy of the limbic system includes the almond-shaped amygdala, the sea–horse shaped hippocampus, the cingulate gyrus that loops around the corpus callosum, and the anterior thalamus and hypothalamus.

As well as dealing with emotions and motivation (it is no coincidence that we link the words in language), the limbic system also plays an important role in developing long-term memory. This explains, in part, why we remember highly charged emotional events more easily than the humdrum details of daily life.

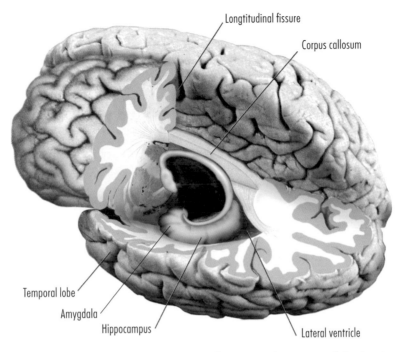

Longtitudinal fissure

Corpus callosum

Temporal lobe

Amygdala

Hippocampus

Lateral ventricle

ABOVE: Revealing the hippocampus in relation to other parts of the brain.

The Cerebellum

Tucked away neatly at the back of the head, the cerebellum ("little brain" in Latin) is crucial for coordination and also seems to influence attention, pleasure, language, and fear. It collects sensory information from the spinal cord and other areas of the brain and uses this data to modulate and fine-tune the body's motor activity.

What's interesting is that damage to the cerebellum does not lead to paralysis. Instead, more subtle movement disorders appear: People can no longer perform rapidly alternating movements (like switching between clapping alternately with the palms and then the backs of their hands) and they have trouble adjusting motor function to sensory stimuli. An example of this is to repeatedly touch one's nose then someone else's finger back and forth, back and forth. If the opposite person moves the finger each time, most people can keep up with a reasonable level of accuracy. Someone with cerebellar damage, however, will be unable to complete this relatively simple task.

The Brain Stem

The brain stem is the most primitive—and the most essential—part of the brain. It consists of the medulla oblongata, the pons, and the midbrain (mesencephalon) and is responsible for keeping us breathing, regulating our heart rate, waking us up, and letting us go back to sleep again. It continues from the spinal cord into the skull, meaning that all channels of motor and sensory information between the rest of the body and the brain must pass through it.

Are You Awake?

From the medulla to the midbrain and thalamus, a loosely organized zone of gray matter, known as the reticular formation, modulates our state of consciousness and level of arousal. Blood flow to the Reticular Activating System (RAS) increases during intense concentration, and the RAS is in turn stimulated by huge sensory signals such as loud noises and cold showers. The RAS also plays an important part in sleep, a process that proceeds through ninety-minute cycles in five distinct stages.

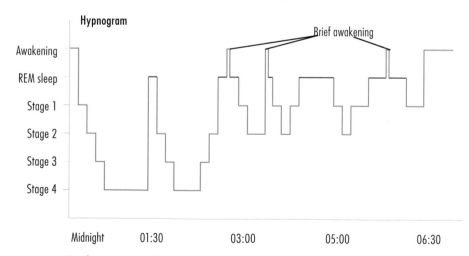

ABOVE: The five stages of sleep based on electrical traces of brain activity, where stage four is the deepest sleep known. Note that rapid-eye-movement (REM) sleep and the arrival of sweet—and not-so-sweet—dreams typically follow a period of deep sleep.

Different Memories and Where They Live

Even after centuries of dedicated research, scientists are still not convinced that we wholly understand memory. The clearest model, proposed by Atkinson and Shiffrin in 1968 (with a few tweaks thereafter), goes as follows:

A sensory register feeds into a short-term store (working memory). This register doesn't forward every piece of information the body can detect, but works as a buffer to protect us from complete and utter sensory overload. Information only reaches the short-term store if we are "paying attention" to it. This short-term store can also access long-term memory stores, but it can only hold around seven chunks of information there at any one time. (By no coincidence, this is the length of an average phone number.)

Information only reaches our long-term memory stores if we "rehearse" it in some way. It seems that our brains have limitless space when it comes to long-term memory. However, the information in the long-term store can decay over time. Long-term memory strengthens each time the short-term store accesses it and new connections are made.

Explicit Memory

Long-term memory is a broad term that covers several different components, including episodic memory (do you remember when Fred wore that clown costume?) and semantic memory (you know what the word "clown" means, but not how you learned it). Together, they make up what researchers call explicit memory. Implicit memory refers to the learning of a task to perform, such as tying shoelaces or serving a tennis ball.

Sport and Traumatic Brain Injury

Initial reports suggest that there is a link between the incidence of head trauma and the risk of dementia later in life. Chronic traumatic encephalopathy is a term that is applied postmortem, when the degenerative changes can be witnessed, along with the build up of a protein called tau. People affected by the condition can experience memory loss, aggression, and depression years, if not decades, after the original head injuries took place.

FACT
Clearly, a strong enough blow to the head can cause irreparable damage on the spot. But in recent years, attention has also been directed at examining the effects of repetitive mild head trauma in contact sports such as boxing, American football, and wrestling.

People Who "Talk and Die"
The case of Natasha Richardson, an actress who died following a fall on a beginners' ski slope, brought widespread attention to the pathophysiology of extradural hematomas. These are collections of blood (hematomas) that develop outside the outermost layer of the meninges that surround the brain (the dura), but inside the skull. The initial impact can be enough to cause a temporary loss of consciousness. Recovery from the initial daze (the so-called talking phase) can mask internal bleeding in the extradural space. As more space fills with blood, the brain is squeezed against the skull and brain damage occurs. Without urgent medical and surgical intervention, this condition becomes fatal. It is for this reason that doctors advise the controlled monitoring of patients following head injuries for symptoms suggestive of raised intracranial pressure, which include drowsiness and vomiting.

5

NERVES AND THE SPINAL CORD

How Nerves Talk

All this thinking, all this running and jumping, all these thrills and reflexes, and shivering… How does the nervous system make it all happen? Through spreading electrical impulses, that's how. Neurons—or nerve cells—consist of a cell body with a nucleus and, typically, a long fiber (axon) that runs between the spinal cord and the final tissue it stimulates or inhibits. At the end of the axon are delicate branching dendritic processes. The microscopic gaps between the dendrites and their targets (nerve, muscle, or tissue) are called synapses. An electrical impulse spreads along the axon to the dendrites to release neurotransmitter chemicals from their storage bubbles. The neurotransmitters travel across the synapse to bind to receptors and trigger another reaction. Neurons in the brain and spinal cord don't always have axons, but they still excite or inhibit the neurons they connect to through synapses.

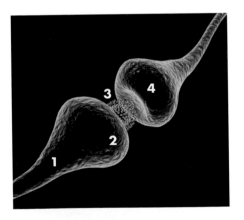

LEFT: A demonstration of the way in which electrical impulses travel from one neuron to another.

1 An electrical impulse travels along the nerve to the synapse (gap).

2 The electricity triggers the release of chemical neurotransmitters.

3 The neurotransmitters diffuse across the gap.

4 Neurotransmitters bind to receptors in the target tissue to either excite or inhibit the tissue.

Myelin: Keeping Things Going

Just like electrical wires, axons need insulation to prevent the electrical charge from decaying over long distances. The human body provides this in the form of myelin, a fat-based substance secreted by surrounding Schwann cells. Unmyelinated fibers, such as those that transmit pain and temperature, transmit their information slowly. Myelin provides for fast transmission—crucial for motor fibers and discriminatory sensory feedback, which can travel at 395 feet (120 meters) per second. Gaps in the myelin sheath called the Nodes of Ranvier allow for a boost in the electrochemical charge through a high concentration of voltage-gated sodium channels in the axonal membrane. Myelin damage results in profound neurological disease, the most common of which is multiple sclerosis.

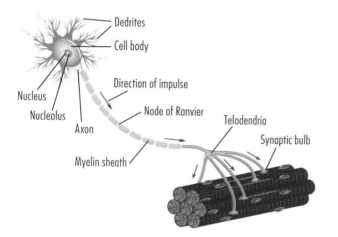

Dedrites
Cell body
Nucleus
Direction of impulse
Nucleolus
Node of Ranvier
Telodendria
Axon
Synaptic bulb
Myelin sheath

LEFT: A diagram illustrating the neuromuscular junction, which connects a body's nervous system to its muscular system.

Nerves themselves are bundles of insulated neurons wrapped up in a sheath called the epineurium. While individual neurons cannot be seen with the naked eye, nerves are visible during surgery and dissection and can even be felt, as in the case of the ulnar nerve at the elbow.

The Simplest Neuronal Arc

As a quick way of analyzing neurological health, doctors often "check reflexes," such as the knee-jerk response. The hammer alters the tension in the tendon, triggering proprioceptive receptors to send an electrical impulse to the spinal cord. A single synapse connects the sensory fiber to a motor fiber, which, in turn, triggers muscle contraction. Under normal conditions, this prevents us from falling over by compensating for the movement and returning our body to its usual position. At the receiving end of a tendon hammer, it causes our leg to jolt upward. This simple exchange at the level of the spinal cord is not only fast, but it also spares the brain from an overload of information. After all, none of us want to spend our days just thinking about sitting up and walking around: one lapse in concentration and we'd fall down. Another, more complicated, reflex can be seen in our eyes. A bright pinpoint of light shone into the pupil will cause it to constrict. Again, this is fast and requires no thought.

Reflex Override *Interestingly, some reflex arcs can be overridden. Concentration (and tension of other muscles) can inhibit the transmission of the knee-jerk reflex, because other neurons inhibit the exchange at the level of the spinal cord. Conversely, your pupils will betray you every time a torch appears. And your pupils will still react when you experience a particularly intense emotion...*

FACT

Ask someone to focus on your finger as you move it toward his or her nose. You will witness another reflex in action (called accommodation): Both pupils constrict as the object in focus becomes closer.

Do Athletes Have Faster Reflexes?

At first, the answer seems obvious: yes. "Keep your eye on the ball," we are told and when it comes to watching Rafael Nadal return a serve in tennis, it's tempting to believe he has faster reflexes than most. However, this is not the case. Instead, Nadal looks into the future.

Experiments involving athletes and nonathletes have determined that we all have similar response times to visual stimuli. When asked to press a button in response to the flash of light on a screen, we hit our limit at around one-fifth of a second. The light must trigger the photoreceptors in our eyes; those signals must be sent on to the visual cortex for processing; we must recognize it as something we need to respond to, make a decision, and send a set of instructions along the motor pathways to our hand. It sounds like quite an accomplishment to race through all of that in only one-fifth of a second.

Predicting the Future *However, when star tennis players are serving at 125 miles (200 km) an hour that only leaves one-third of a second to get into position and swing. In other words, not enough time. The only way to return a serve like that is to predict the ball's flight path before it is struck. And that's just what elite players do. Using key signals from body position and racket movement learned through years of practice, pro tennis stars can accurately identify where a ball will go. Experiments show that they can even make the same correct judgment call when body position is reduced to a series of points in space rather than the actual figure of an opposing player.*

Learned Cues *Such skills seem sport specific, however. Female softball pitcher Jennie Finch repeatedly struck out major league baseball pros even though she was pitching at a slower speed than they were used to and using a larger ball. Why? Because they had learned different cues and, like the rest of us, simply couldn't respond fast enough in the face of this new information.*

The Spinal Cord

The spinal cord continues from the medulla oblongata (the lower part of the brain stem) at the level of the foramen magnum (large hole) at the base of the skull. It runs through the spinal canal created by the vertebrae until it reaches the level of the first lumbar vertebra. After that, it tapers into an inverted cone called the conus medullaris. The thread–like filum terminale then extends from the conus medullaris down to attach to the coccyx. Nerve roots fill the remainder of the spinal canal, giving the appearance of a horse's tail and thus earning themselves the name of cauda equina ("horse's tail" in Latin.)

Along the length of the spinal cord run pairs of roots. The front (anterior) roots supply motor commands and the back (posterior) roots relay sensory information. These nerve roots pass through their respective intervertebral foramina (holes) to unite to form the spinal nerves. These spinal nerves then diverge and recombine to form peripheral nerves through networks called plexuses.

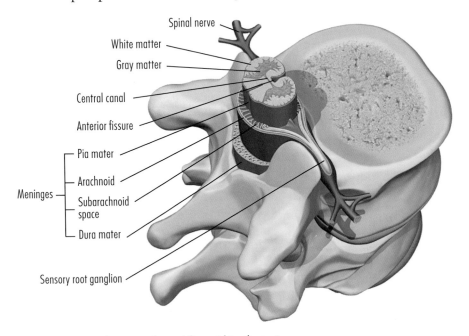

Spinal nerve

White matter

Gray matter

Central canal

Anterior fissure

Pia mater

Arachnoid

Meninges

Subarachnoid space

Dura mater

Sensory root ganglion

ABOVE: How the spinal cord fits within the spine.

Spinal Trauma

The catastrophic aftermath of spinal trauma and nerve injuries results from the extremely limited ability of neuronal tissue to regenerate. Whereas cells in the gastrointestinal (GI) tract and skin can divide and regenerate easily, the cell bodies of neurons are so specialized that they cannot. Some degree of healing, however, is possible. Axons can regrow along their original tracts if the scaffolding remains intact and if the supporting cells (glia) are healthy and able to provide support. Schwann cells and macrophages (a type of white blood cell) clear the debris of the farthest part of the nerve and produce molecules such as laminin and fibronectin to enhance the growth of the part of the axon closest to the cell body (the proximal stump). Not surprisingly, research continues into ways of enhancing this scaffolding with biosynthetic products as well as seeking other factors that could enhance nerve regrowth following injury.

Phantom Pain *During the French military campaigns of the mid-sixteenth century, royal surgeon Ambroise Paré noted that soldiers frequently continued to sense pain long after an amputation had healed. The phenomenon is known to this day. In such cases, transected nerve endings heal well enough to continue sending signals to the spinal cord, so giving information to the brain that the missing limb is not only there, but that it hurts. Even years after the initial injury, amputees report sensations of itch, warmth, and heaviness coming from a limb that is no longer there.*

ABOVE: Ambroise Paré—the first person to document phantom limb syndrome in a patient.

Skin

Often overlooked, the skin is the largest organ in the body, comprising a surprising 16 percent of our total body weight. It protects us from the harsh realities of the world—heat, cold, water, friction, radiation, and smoke—and then reflects those realities through pigment spots and wrinkles. It's only 0.02 inches (0.5 mm) thick on our eyelids and up to 1/8 inch (5 mm) thick on the soles of our feet. It can be stretchy, soft, and splotchy, yet it replaces its surface entirely every twenty-eight to thirty days.

The epidermis sits on the surface, the dermis beneath it, and the hypodermis beneath that. The epidermis itself consists of five layers, from outer to inner: the stratum corneum, the stratum licidum, the stratum granulosum, the stratum spinosum, and the stratum basale. Cells divide in the stratum basale, pushing the cells above them out toward the world. As cells progress through these layers, they flatten and die before they are shed.

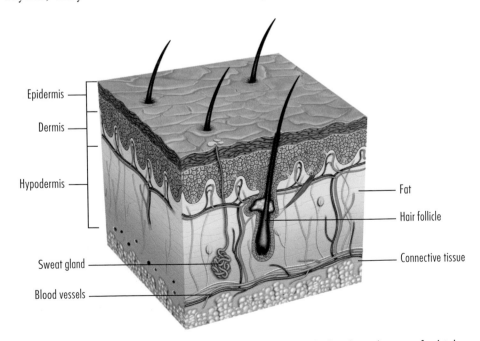

ABOVE: A cross-section through the human skin reveals the three layers of which it is composed: the epidermis, the dermis, and the hypodermis.

Touch

Pacinian corpuscles are nerve endings wrapped in onion-like layers of connective tissue in the skin. They respond to vibration and pressure because any deformation of the capsule causes sodium channels to open in the membrane of the axon. This leads to a rapid influx of positive ions, which triggers an action potential along the nerve. Other

ABOVE: A Pacinian corpuscle seen under the microscope.

mechanoreceptors function in a similar way, such as Merkel cells and Meissner's corpuscles, which respond to light touch.

Thermoreceptors, meanwhile, do not appear to have specialized structures but rely, instead, on simple nerve endings. There are separate populations for detecting the sensations of cold and warmth and their method of transmission is not yet fully understood.

Touchy–Feely *The tactile sensitivity of skin is directly proportional to the number of sensory receptors in an area and the overlap of their respective receptive fields. Our fingertips have the best sense of touch with the lowest two-point discrimination (the ability to feel two separate objects distinctly, even when they are placed close together). That's because they have the highest concentration of sensory receptors with small overlapping receptive fields.*

Proprioception

The Latin word *proprio* means "one's own" and it relates to knowing which part of our leg is where, so that we can walk in the dark, or where our fingers are when we pick something up so that we don't crush it. In roadside drunk-driving tests, it means being able to touch the end of the own nose with the eyes closed, since alcohol intoxication impairs proprioception and balance.

Proprioceptors are scattered throughout the body. In tendons, proprioceptive Golgi tendon organs are interwoven between fibers. Within muscles there are sensory muscle spindles alongside the actin and myosin. Information from these organs, together with proprioceptors in the skin and vestibular neurons in the semicircular canals of the ear, combine to let us know both consciously and unconsciously where we are and what we're doing.

Friction Blisters

Repetitive friction forces on the skin lead to a separation of cells within the epidermis at the level of the stratum spinosum. Plasma-like fluid fills the potential space, causing the whitened, fluid-filled pouch we all know. After around twenty-four hours, cells in the basal layer begin to divide and the stratum granulosum and stratum corneum are replaced within 48 to 120 hours respectively. To prevent infection and reduce pain, it's recommended to keep the "roof" of the blister in place. Despite numerous trials into what kind of footwear prevents blister formation, science is still waiting for the single definitive answer.

FACT
Described as technological doping after every swimming gold medal at the Beijing Olympics went to an athlete in a LZR (pronounced laser) racer suit, new fibers proved faster in the water than skin. Wearers smashed over 130 world records before a ban was introduced in 2010.

Reducing Drag

Interestingly, there's little evidence to support the ritual shaving of swimmers and cyclists (although little doesn't mean none). While cyclists shave primarily to make it easier to clean their wounds and to lessen the tarmac tearing chunks from their skin, in the world of swimming it's all about reducing friction in the pool.

6

SIGHT
SOUND
SMELL
TASTE

Miraculous Sight

If a picture paints a thousand words, that's nothing compared to what the photoreceptors of the eye can do. With over 190 million photoreceptors and the ability to see starlight millions of light years away—but also a tiny hair growing on the back of a human hand—the power of human sight is truly an extraordinary thing. And it all begins in the eye.

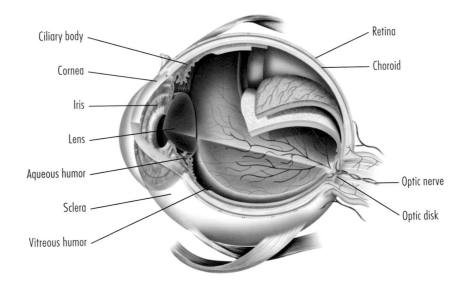

ABOVE: This cross-section of the human eye reveals the parts that make vision possible in relation to one another.

Inside the Orbit

Home to the eyeball, the orbit is shaped more like a pyramid than a sphere, with its base facing out to the world and its apex digging back into the skull. Seven pairs of extraocular muscles hold the eyeball in position: the levator palpebrae superioris, superior rectus, inferior rectus, lateral rectus, medial rectus, and superior and inferior obliques. The lacrimal gland sits in the upper outer part of the orbit, shedding tears through twelve or more ducts that spill out onto the surface of the eye (the conjunctiva).

The Eye Itself *The eyeball sits within the bony orbit and is cushioned by supportive orbital fat. It has a fibrous coat with a white part (the sclera) and a transparent part (the cornea). The optic nerve pierces the sclera at the back of the eyeball in an area called the lamina cribrosa. This area of weakness can bulge into the eyeball if the intracranial pressure increases, leading to a subtle sign of "cupping" that can be seen when looking through the pupil using an ophthalmoscope.*

Inside the eyeball, the aqueous humor fills the front chamber of the eye, the vitreous humor fills the back, and the lens sits in between. The ciliary body produces the aqueous humor and alters the shape of the lens to allow you to focus. The iris has muscles of its own that constrict or dilate the pupil, thereby altering the amount of light that enters the eye.

Mapping Out the Retina

The retina has an outer pigmented layer and an inner nervous layer lined with photoreceptors. These receptors earn their names (rods or cones) on account of their appearance under an electron microscope. Rods can detect extremely low levels of light (such as the Andromeda galaxy 2.6 million light years away). Cones, however, require more light but can detect color and fine detail.

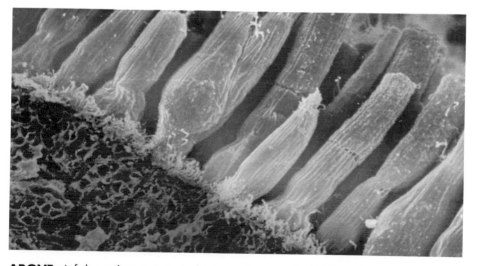

ABOVE: A false-color scanning electron micrograph (SEM) to show rod (blue) and cone (green-blue) cells of the retina.

How Eyes Reveal Emotion

Are the eyes the windows to the soul? Well, they do offer the only way of looking straight at the brain (the optic nerve and retinal cells develop as direct outgrowths of the brain).

Then there's the pupil, which not only changes size in response to ambient light, but responds to emotions as well. Firing of the flight or fight response (the sympathetic nervous system) leads to pupil dilation. This is because the body needs as much light as possible in order to sense someone or something about to attack. When the opposing, parasympathetic nervous system fires, (the "chill out man, have some soda" kind of response) the pupil constricts—just like a pinhole camera—to provide less light but better focus. What's even more interesting is that these changes occur without any real threat. Showing students photos of dead bodies or scantily clad models will cause their pupils to dilate ... but so, too, will complicated arithmetic! Finally, there's the theory that we look away when we lie. So, emotion, mental effort, and truth—that's a lot more than just vision.

Central and Peripheral Vision

Central vision is processed by the macula of the retina—that is, the part that we direct our gaze toward. Within the macula, the concentration of rods and cones is greater than at the periphery. The area with the highest concentration of cones is called the fovea—that's where visual acuity is at its greatest.

Peripheral vision refers to the blurry sight provided by the rods toward the edge of our field of view. We rely on this when trying to sense what's going on around us. It is crucial in team sports like hockey as well as in solo sports where it's important to monitor a competitor's movements.

How We Hear

Although sound conveys complicated speech and subtle, orchestral beauty, it also evokes a primitive startle response. Even people with cortical deafness (who cannot consciously hear) will jump at an unexpected loud noise, thanks to the startle response elicited by a neural pathway older in evolutionary terms. It should come as no surprise, therefore, that sound starts many a sporting competition, be it a whistle, a buzzer, or a shot.

Anatomy of the Ear

The part of the ear we can see is called the external ear. The auricle is the elastic cartilage covered by skin and the external auditory meatus is the tube that leads to the eardrum (tympanic membrane). Behind the tympanic membrane lies the tympanic cavity or middle ear, an air-filled area encased in the petrous part of the temporal bone. It contains the smallest bones in the body—commonly referred to as the hammer, anvil, and stirrup (the malleus, incus, and stapes, collectively known as the auditory ossicles). These

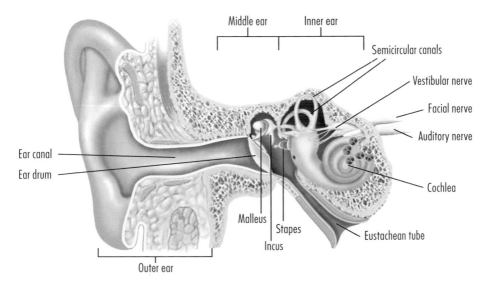

ABOVE: This cutaway diagram demonstrates just how much of the human ear is invisible to the eye.

auditory ossicles amplify the vibrations of the tympanic membrane by a factor of twenty, transmitting that energy to the oval window that connects to the vestibule of the inner ear.

Within the inner ear lie the fluid-filled cochlea and semicircular canals. The cochlea, a snail-shaped organ, transmits waves from the ossicles at the oval window along the length of the basilar membrane that runs inside it. The round window bulges back into the middle ear in accordance with the pulsing of the oval window to allow the fluid within the cochlea to move.

That movement stimulates stereocilia cells on the basilar membrane known as the Organ of Corti. The hairlike structure of these cells converts vibrations into electrical impulses that travel, ultimately, along the vestibulocochlear nerve (cranial nerve VIII) and on to the auditory processing centers of the brain.

Balance

The inner ear also contains the semicircular canals—fluid-filled hoops that detect motion along three different axes (pitch, roll, and yaw.) That information, combined with proprioceptive feedback that travels along the spinal cord, keeps us in balance, even when our eyes are closed.

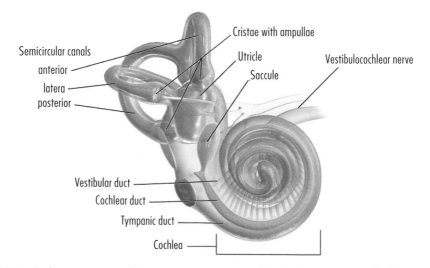

ABOVE: A close-up view of the inner ear, responsible for keeping us in balance.

A Sense of Smell

One of the most striking things to learn about the nose is that the nasal passage doesn't go "up" along the visible contours of the nose, but straight back, parallel to the roof of the mouth. The part of the nose we can see has a bony root, then a distal cartilaginous structure, and a central septum.

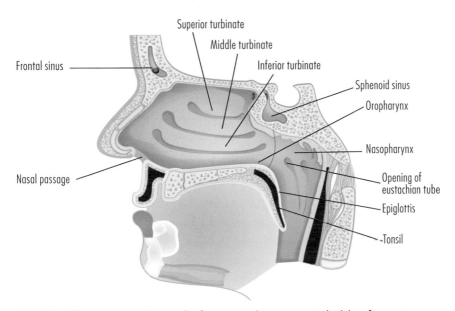

ABOVE: Like the ear, almost all of our nasal anatomy is hidden from view.

Inside the nose are three nasal conchae: bony protrusions covered with mucosal tissue, which provide a large surface-area-to-volume ratio, to warm and moisten air as it enters. Hairs at the entrance to the nasal passage also prevent debris from reaching the airways. The nasal cavity receives openings from various sinuses of the skull (the sphenoidal, posterior ethmoidal, maxillary, frontal and anterior ethmoidal) as well as the nasolacrimal duct. The nasolacrimal duct runs from the eye to the nose. Its function is to empty excess tears into the nose. That's why if you've been crying for a while, you'll feel the need to blow your nose...

FACT
Applying pressure at the top of the nose during a nosebleed does nothing to stem the flow of blood. This bony part of the nose cannot be compressed. Instead, pressure should be applied to the lower, softer part of the nose in order to facilitate clot formation.

The Oldest Sense in the World

A human's sense of smell is the oldest sense in the history of mammals and in biological terms we still use it to seek food and influence social and sexual behavior (think baking, deodorant, and eau de cologne). It starts at the olfactory mucous membrane, which lines the superior concha and sphenoethmoidal recess in the upper part of the nose. Olfactory nerve fibers pass straight through the cribiform plate of the skull to the brain. The olfactory nerve is the first cranial nerve (one of twelve pairs that arise directly from the brain instead of from the spinal cord).

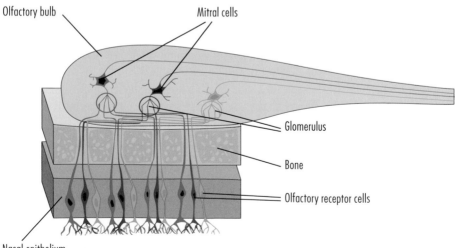

Olfactory bulb
Mitral cells
Glomerulus
Bone
Olfactory receptor cells
Nasal epithelium

ABOVE: A close-up of the olfactory bulb, showing how we transmit smells to the brain, from fragrances to garbage.

Taste, Teeth, and Saliva

It brings us pleasure, it revolts us, and apparently there's no accounting for it! Taste may be one of the least "critical" senses we have, but life would surely be less interesting without it.

All the flavors of the world, from sumptuous chocolate cake to off-putting cod liver oil, are thought to derive from five basic tastes: salt, sweet, sour, bitter, and umami (the "amino acid" flavor of monosodium glutamate.) In actual fact, taste itself makes up less than 50 percent of the experience of flavor. Olfactory input from the nose carries almost as much weight, with sight and sound contributing, too.

The Tongue

The tongue is a mass of muscle covered with mucous membrane. The front two-thirds sit in the mouth, the final third in the throat (pharynx). The tongue has intrinsic muscles (those not attached to bone) as well as extrinsic ones that attach to bones and the soft palate (genioglossus, hyoglossus, styloglossus, and palatoglossus). The oral part of the tongue has numerous papillae (which you can see directly) and taste buds, or neuroepithelial receptor cells (which you can't).

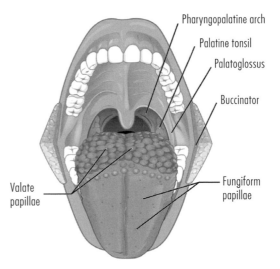

Pharyngopalatine arch

Palatine tonsil

Palatoglossus

Buccinator

Fungiform papillae

Valate papillae

ABOVE: The human tongue seen face on. The diagram demonstrates the location of the palatoglossus tongue muscles and papillae.

Teeth

As adults, we have thirty-two teeth (four incisors, two canines, four premolars, and six molars in each jaw). These replace our twenty deciduous (milk) teeth. Adult teeth grow in the jaw before the deciduous teeth fall out.

Taking a Bite

Our biting and chewing mechanisms take place thanks to a group of muscles known as the muscles of mastication. These muscles originate across the skull and attach to the mandible (jaw), allowing them to affect its movement. The small medial ptyerygoid, the superficial temporalis, and the strong masseter muscles snap our jaws shut. The lateral pterygoid opens the jaw, with assistance from smaller muscles that attach to the hyoid bone.

By alternating which muscles of mastication we use, we can move our jaw from side to side in order to chew. Although these four muscles get all the credit for biting and chewing, many others—the intrinsic muscles of the tongue and the facial muscles that control the lips, for example—are required in order for us to eat and swallow successfully.

What is saliva? *Saliva is a watery substance that keeps the mouth and throat healthy and happy. Digestive enzymes tackle remnants of food stuck between the teeth when we eat, while water and mucus keep everything lubricated. Saliva also contains an antibody that fights infection (Immunoglobulin or IgA), as well as other antimicrobial substances such as lysozyme and lactoferrin. Not only do these protect the oral cavity, they also augment healing when it comes (literally) to licking our wounds.*

7

CHEMICAL CONTROL

The Science of Satisfaction

While your mind and countless advertising campaigns may urge you to strive for bigger, better, faster, the chemical system within your body tends to have a different aim: to stay the same. The term homeostasis refers to the attempt to maintain equilibrium between interdependent elements, and it applies to many physiological systems in the human body: temperature, pH, blood volume, salt concentrations, energy levels, and sleep patterns.

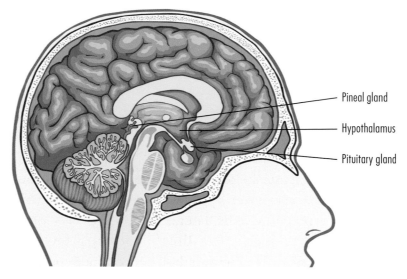

Pineal gland

Hypothalamus

Pituitary gland

ABOVE: Very small parts of the human brain, yet crucial components of the endocrine system—the pineal gland, the pituitary gland, and the hypothalamus.

The Endocrine System

Endocrinology is the study of the endocrine system through which substances are secreted into the blood (rather than into other systems) in order to influence tissue function elsewhere. These substances are called hormones and most hormones are inextricably linked to two small parts of the brain:

- *The pituitary gland*
- *The hypothalamus*

The bean-shaped pituitary gland occupies a bony recess at the center of the base of the skull. Its posterior lobe receives nerve endings from the hormone-producing hypothalamus, another part of the brain, while its anterior lobe produces a range of hormones itself. Between them, they coordinate a wide range of bodily functions that include hunger, sleep, reproduction, libido, growth, childbirth, beards, and breast size.

FACT
Experiments suggest that for athletic endeavors, accuracy and complex strategy planning peak in the morning, whereas strength at repetitive exercise reaches its peak later in the day.

Hunger: When Is Enough Enough?
Until recently, scientists believed that hunger control could be explained by the "dual center hypothesis." According to this, one part of the hypothalamus (the lateral hypothalamus) stimulates hunger sensations in response to falling blood sugar levels and an empty stomach. A second (ventromedial) part of the hypothalamus, then stimulates the feeling of having eaten enough (satiety) in response to rising blood sugar levels, an extended stomach, and other feedback mechanisms. However, today, a more popular explanation is that of a "set point." Here, hunger and satiety are modulated in response an individual's body weight, and aim always to take the body back to its own set point.

Eating Disorders *Research continues to explore the realm of hunger as humanity attempts to deal with one of the paradoxes of history: Despite having more information relating to diet and better nutrition available than ever before, the rates of eating disorders (both anorexia nervosa and obesity) are the highest ever seen.*

The Circadian Rhythm: Why We Get Jet Lag

Shift workers and jet-set travelers know only too well that the "body clock" has a mechanism that is only partially responsive to willpower. A circadian rhythm (from the Latin *circa*—around, *diem*—day) refers to the pattern of bodily processes that are organized around a period of just over twenty-four hours. Among the processes that take place during this period are the following:

- *The steroid hormone cortisol surges in the morning*
- *Body temperature decreases overnight*
- *The pineal gland in the brain secretes melatonin from dusk until dawn*
- *Even heart attacks seem affected by the time of day, with a peak in the early hours of the morning*

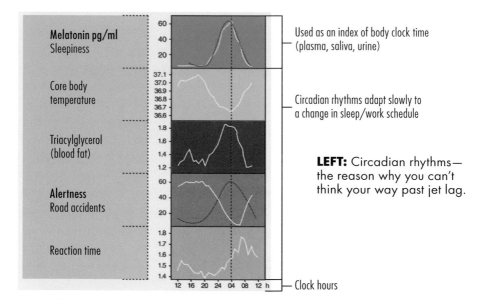

Melatonin pg/ml
Sleepiness

Core body temperature

Triacylglycerol (blood fat)

Alertness
Road accidents

Reaction time

Used as an index of body clock time (plasma, saliva, urine)

Circadian rhythms adapt slowly to a change in sleep/work schedule

LEFT: Circadian rhythms— the reason why you can't think your way past jet lag.

Clock hours

The body's key "biological clock" is believed to be the suprachiasmatic nuclei (SCN) of the hypothalamus. This area of the brain receives information about light from specialized photoreceptors in the retina, as well as chemical cues from the blood and information from the brain about social and environmental conditions. (For example: I feel so tired but I have to stay awake because of this work presentation/I'm at the wheel/it would be embarrassing to go to bed now.)

FACT
A woman's core body temperature increases just after ovulation (following the production of the temperature-rising hormone progesterone) and throughout pregnancy.

Thermoregulation

Core body temperature is tightly controlled to within around 0.9 degrees of 98.6°F (0.5 degrees of 37°C). A temperature of 100.4°F (38°C) and above indicates fever; below 96.8°F (36°C) indicates hypothermia. Peripheral body temperature can vary more wildly, as anyone who comes into contact with a woman's feet in the months of winter can attest.

Such strict temperature control is required to allow the body's enzymes to function correctly and to avoid these proteins, as well as the phospholipids and lipoproteins of cell membranes, becoming "denatured" or liquefying (imagine a clear, liquid egg white becoming a rubbery hard white structure).

The Body's Thermostat

The hypothalamus coordinates heat gains, losses, and maintenance. Our body produces heat through metabolic activity, even at rest, which it can increase by running or shivering and decrease by lying still. Our behavior can also raise our temperature—for example, by sitting in the sun (radiation), sitting by a radiator (convection), and sitting on a hot-water bottle (conduction.) We can also lose heat by each of these methods—sitting on a cold metal chair would transfer body heat to the chair.

Besides our behavior, we also have a range of automatic modes of thermoregulation. Dilating and constricting the blood vessels in the skin (cutaneous vasodilation and vasoconstriction, respectively) can powerfully modulate heat exchange, while sweat loses heat through evaporation. Piloerection—when our hairs stand on end—traps air close to the skin to conserve heat.

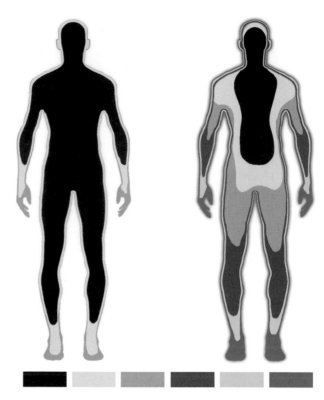

RIGHT: An illustration to show the distribution of body heat. Under normal situations (left), the hands, feet, and scrotum are slightly cooler than the core. As hypothermia develops, the body sacrifices heat in the peripheries to maintain a stable core temperature (right).

Hypothermia and Exposure *When a newspaper reports that someone "died from exposure," it usually means that the person died from hypothermia. This can happen during surprisingly mild conditions, particularly in the elderly or in those who are intoxicated or immobile for various reasons. But even experienced hikers and mountaineers can succumb to hypothermia if their mechanisms for generating heat cannot overcome their losses.*

As body temperature falls, the heart muscle becomes less able to conduct electricity. This reduces the heart rate, which in turn reduces the blood supply to the rest of the body. Consequently, the ability to generate heat through shivering or through behavior (putting on more clothes, walking to safety, calling for help) falls as well. The configuration of hemoglobin changes, making it less likely to release oxygen even at this great time of need. Brain function declines, leading to increasingly erratic behavior and decisions that can be mistaken for intoxication or stroke.

Heat Stroke and Heat Exhaustion *Of the various heat-related illnesses, heat stroke is the most severe. Children and the elderly are vulnerable during heat waves, and athletes and military recruits are at increased risk during periods of intense training. Heat stroke is also a risk of stimulant drugs such as cocaine, ecstasy, and amphetamine.*

Heat exhaustion is less severe, but it can progress to heat stroke. Headache, nausea, dizziness, and vomiting often occur. Neurological symptoms, such as convulsions, abnormal gait, or decreased levels of consciousness are indicative of heat stroke and are a medical emergency.

FACT

At rest, our body produces approximately 1 kcal/kg/h. Without cooling mechanisms, this can raise core body temperature by 1.98°F/h (1.1°C/h). Intense exercise can increase heat production more than ten-fold.

Growth Hormone

One of the many products of the anterior pituitary gland is growth hormone (also known as hGH, where the first h signifies "human"). Growth hormone stimulates the production of IGF-1 (insulin-like growth factor) by the liver, which in turn stimulates cartilage, muscle, and bone growth. Growth hormone also increases the effects of anabolic steroids and, as such, is a banned substance in competitive sports. Its use can lead to a number of conditions, including diabetes, high blood pressure, joint pain, and accelerated wear and tear of the joints (osteoarthritis).

Acromegaly is the name of the medical condition that occurs when too much growth hormone is produced after puberty. Patients develop abnormally large hands and feet, a prominent tongue, and exaggerated facial features. They cannot become taller, however, because their bones have already fused.

How Kidneys Work

The kidneys comprise less than 0.5 percent of our body weight and yet they receive 25 percent of our cardiac output. Each minute, they take 2 3/4 pints (1300 ml) of blood via the renal arteries and produce only half a teaspoon of urine. We have two, just in case, and they're one of the few organs whose functions we can mimic through the use of machines over a sustained period of time.

The Importance of Urine

The principal function of the kidneys is the production of urine—a rather unexciting fluid that consists of water, salt, some acid, and waste products like urea. But the impressive part of kidney function is its role in maintaining both the volume and concentration of the blood. The gastrointestinal tract aims to absorb whatever it can. The kidneys then decide what to keep.

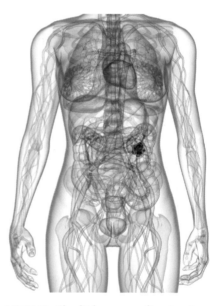

ABOVE: The kidneys are fist-sized organs that sit high in the abdomen, protected by the rib cage.

Each kidney has more than one million nephrons, and each nephron contains a Bowman's capsule in the cortex and a tubule that loops deep into the medulla before returning to the cortex to empty its contents into a collecting tubule.

The kidneys produce urine by both filtering fluid from the blood and actively secreting waste products. Most of the filtered fluid is reabsorbed according to the needs of the body, along with other useful substances, such as glucose.

How Does the Body Keep its Blood in Balance?

First through keeping a constant concentration of salt (sodium chloride—NaCl), then by adjusting the total volume of salty fluid. It works like this: The hypothalamus produces an antidiuretic hormone (ADH), which it stores in the posterior pituitary gland. As plasma osmolality increases (principally as NaCl concentrations rise), ADH is released. It acts on the kidney to increase water reabsorption through channels in the collecting ducts and distal convoluted tubules (DCTs) of the nephron. The increased water reabsorption restores plasma osmolality, but may increase overall blood volume. Another hormone that affects salt balance in the kidneys is aldosterone, produced by the zona glomerulosa of the adrenal gland. It increases sodium reabsorption in the kidney at the expense of potassium, while also increasing water reabsorption and blood pressure.

Marathon Hazard *Hydration should be balanced carefully in marathon runners in order to avoid a salt imbalance in the blood (a condition called dilutional hyponatraemia). If electrolyte-rich fluid is lost through sweat, but only water is ingested, NaCl levels in the blood risk falling to dangerous levels, causing seizures.*

After Salt, Water: The Renin-Angiotensin System

When blood volume falls, juxtaglomerular cells in the kidneys respond by secreting renin, which sets off a series of chain reactions. Renin converts angiotensinogen from the liver into angiotensin I. Angiotensin I is converted into angiotensin II by ACE (angiotensin converting enzyme) in the lungs. Thus activated, angiotensin II causes powerful vasoconstriction as well as triggering aldosterone release from the adrenal glands. The sheer number of steps and organs involved in this process provide ample opportunities for pharmaceutical interventions to try to lower an individual's pathologically high blood pressure.

How We Breathe

It's curious that, while few of us can control our heartbeat, even tiny children can control their breathing. For meditation, diving, and blowing out birthday candles, conscious respiratory control appears to be a useful thing. But what about the rest of the time, when we forget? What keeps the chest moving up and down, the abdomen in and out? And how does the body know whether we're quietly reading a book (like now) or racing toward the finish line?

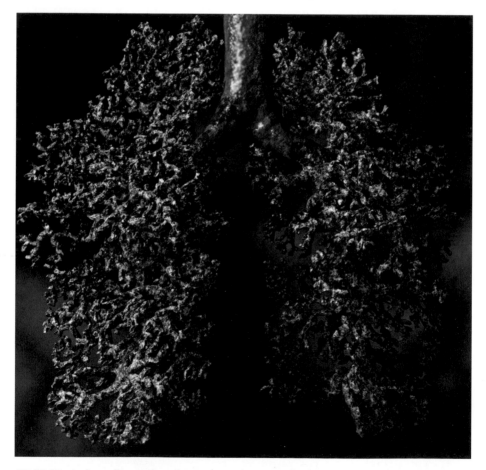

ABOVE: A digitally rendered image to show inside the lungs. The bronchioles branch into ever more delicate structures to maximize gas exchange.

> **FACT**
> We lose more than 1 pint (500 ml) of water and 360 kCal energy in heat each day through evaporation from our respiratory passageways.

Respiratory Triggers

We breathe in through the combined effort of the diaphragm and intercostal muscles, which create a negative pressure within the thorax. This pulls air in; the chest's elastic recoil eases air back out. The exchange of carbon dioxide and oxygen occurs at the level of the capillaries, which wrap themselves around the thin bubbles of the terminal structures of the airways (alveoli).

While cardiac muscle has its own intrinsic rhythm, the skeletal muscle that makes up the diaphragm and intercostal muscle does not. Instead, it relies entirely on the nervous system for a stimulus to contract. The cerebral cortex controls breathing for situations involving singing, speaking, and blowing out candles on a birthday cake; the pons and the medulla in the brainstem keep us alive. Interestingly, it is carbon dioxide rather than oxygen that has the greatest effect on breathing. This is due to its propensity to react with water as follows:

$$CO_2 + H_2O = H{+} + HCO_3{-}$$

So carbon dioxide in the blood has a tendency to make the blood acidic (more hydrogen ions). Central chemoreceptors on the medulla oblongata detect increasing levels of hydrogen and trigger breathing in order to bring them back down. Low levels of oxygen (hypoxia) also stimulate breathing via chemoreceptors in the carotid body and aortic arch. However, the drop in oxygen must be quite significant to trigger a response, so this "back-up plan" is usually only witnessed at high altitude, in patients with lung disease, or from hypoventilation due to other causes.

Maximal Oxygen Consumption

Maximal oxygen consumption (VO_2max) is a frequently used marker of cardiovascular fitness, albeit one that has courted controversy. Physiologically, it follows the Fick Equation:

Maximal oxygen uptake (VO_2max) = Cardiac Output (Stroke Volume × Heart Rate) × arterio-venous oxygen difference

In practice, it is usually calculated through a treadmill protocol where a subject is asked to exercise until exhaustion while breathing through a tube that measures the gases exhaled. The result is expressed as ml/kg/min and reflects the peak volume of oxygen an individual can consume in one minute.

The debate surrounds just what this means. It is already known that, as aerobic fitness increases, so does cardiac output during exercise—through an increase in stroke volume (through the build up of heart muscle) and a decrease in resting heart rate (allowing more scope for it to increase during exercise). The question exists as to whether the limit is truly set by the cardiovascular system (subjects must decide when they are exhausted, after all) and whether or not there are changes at a cellular level that influence oxygen consumption and aerobic metabolism as well.

Athletic VO_2max *Elite endurance athletes have a much higher measured VO_2max than the general population. However, athletes with the highest VO_2max don't necessarily outperform their colleagues during endurance events and some lay people have a VO_2max that would embarrass some highly decorated athletes.*

✳ FACT

The average VO_2max for a twenty-year-old male would be 40 ml/kg/min, 30 ml/kg/min for a female. A thoroughbred racehorse has a VO_2max of 180 ml/kg/min.

Henry's Law

Henry's law states that the solubility of a gas in a liquid is proportional to the pressure of the gas over the solution:

$$P = Hv \star M$$

- *P is the partial pressure of the gas*
- *Hv is the Henry's law proportionality constant*
- *M is the molar concentration of the gas in solution*

At high altitudes, although oxygen concentrations are the same, the partial pressures are lower because atmospheric pressure is lower. Consequently, the concentration of oxygen in the blood is lower. This "relative hypoxia" drives the body to increase its oxygen carrying capacity, most notably through increasing its red blood cell count and thereby hemoglobin concentration. This natural physiological response is very attractive to athletes from higher altitudes who are training to compete in events held at a lower altitude where their increased red blood cell count will give them an advantage against those who train at lower altitudes.

The Bends *Deep below the sea, the partial pressures of gases in the lungs increase, making more gas dissolve in the blood. Nitrogen, which makes up around 78 percent of air, dissolves without causing problems as it is chemically inert. However, as the diver ascends, atmospheric pressure drops. If the ascent is too rapid, the soluble nitrogen becomes gas bubbles again. Even small bubbles can block arteries and arterioles, damaging the tissues they supply. That's why decompression sickness has such a wide variety of symptoms, from headaches to rashes to joint pain, and—ultimately—death.*

Adrenaline, Steroids, and Stress

An adrenal gland sits on top of each kidney, much like a triangular Napoleonic hat. Both glands have an outer cortex and an inner medulla, each of which have a different embryological origin, structure, and function. These glands are involved in the "flight or fight" response.

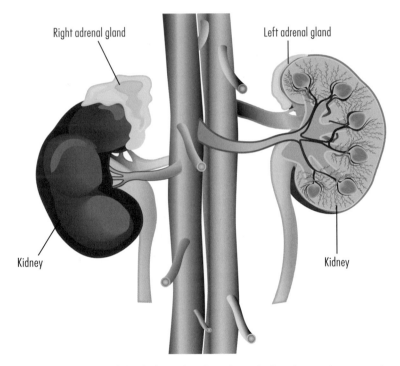

Right adrenal gland

Left adrenal gland

Kidney

Kidney

ABOVE: The positions of the left and right adrenal glands in relation to the kidneys when the body is facing the viewer.

The Medulla

The adrenal medulla secretes adrenaline and noradrenaline, which together are known as catecholamines. They modulate the spectrum of responses between "I'd better sit up and pay more attention" to "I'm running for my life," through receptors located throughout the body. These receptors are broadly organized into alpha and beta groups, with adrenaline stimulating both and noradrenaline mainly stimulating alpha receptors. Together, the catecholamines raise blood pressure, heart rate, and myocardial contractility. They decrease bronchial resistance in the lungs and increase the rate of glycogen breakdown in the liver. They mobilize fat from adipose tissue to provide an alternative energy source, they increase alertness, and dilate pupils to enhance peripheral vision. They also give some a buzz that makes them want to jump out of an airplane again, and again, and again.

Stimulating Beta-receptors *Salbutamol, which stimulates the beta receptors, is a common "reliever" inhaler in asthma. By mimicking the effect of adrenaline, the airways dilate to make breathing easier. The slight overlap with the beta-1 receptors in the heart can also increase the heart rate and make people feel jittery.*

FACT
Anabolic steroids are the ones most often misused for cosmetic and sporting purposes. They resemble the sex steroids rather than the corticosteroids and they build up protein (anabolic) rather than break it apart (catabolic).

Beta-blockers in Sport *Although adrenaline enhances athletic performance in many ways, for precision sports it is more likely to be a hindrance. Adrenaline released under pressure can cause tremors and performance anxiety, both of which can be reduced by taking beta-blocker drugs. As a result, sports like archery, darts, and shooting may have beta-blockers on their list of banned substances.*

The Cortex
The adrenal cortex has three distinct zones. The outer (zona glomerulosa) secretes aldosterone, which modulates salt and water retention by the kidneys. The inner (zona reticularis) produces sex steroids. And the middle part, the (zona fasciculate), produces steroid hormones (glucocorticoids), principally cortisol.

When it comes to stress, the catecholamines work faster but the effects of cortisol last longer. The corticosteroids promote the breakdown (catabolism) of proteins into amino acids to allow those to be used as glucose in the liver. The early discovery of this function is responsible for the generic term glucocorticoids (in contrast to mineralocorticoids such as aldosterone).

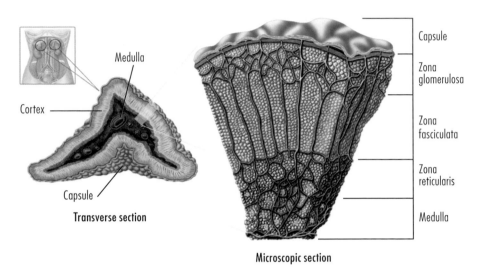

Transverse section

Cortex

Medulla

Capsule

Microscopic section

Capsule

Zona glomerulosa

Zona fasciculata

Zona reticularis

Medulla

ABOVE: The anatomy of the adrenal glands. Each of the different zones produces different substances.

Experiences of cold, fasting, bleeding, surgery, infection, pain, severe exercise, and emotional trauma all cause the hypothalamus in the brain to release CRH (corticotropin–releasing hormone.) This stimulates the release of ACTH from the anterior pituitary gland, which in turn stimulates the adrenal cortex to synthesize and release cortisol.

In addition to its effects on the glucose pathway, cortisol is required for both glucagon and growth hormone to function properly. It promotes wound healing and sets the body's daily rhythm with an early morning pulse. It also tends to put people in a good mood.

8

THE ANATOMY OF DIGESTION

The Digestive System

The journey from one end of our digestive system to the other is one that can last up to fifty hours in healthy adults. It begins in the mouth, where the salivary glands release enzymes to commence digestion and to inform the stomach that food is on its way. After swallowing, food continues into the esophagus.

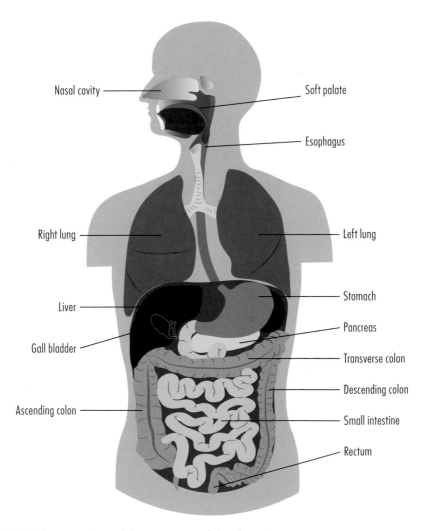

Nasal cavity

Soft palate

Esophagus

Right lung

Left lung

Liver

Stomach

Gall bladder

Pancreas

Transverse colon

Descending colon

Ascending colon

Small intestine

Rectum

ABOVE: An overview of the anatomy of the digestive system.

The Esophagus

The entire gastrointestinal (GI) tract begins as a single tube during embryology, with various parts budding off, expanding, or looping to form organs, such as the liver, pancreas, gallbladder, and so on. The esophagus, however, doesn't loop, bud, or expand too much. It remains a simple muscular tube that carries food from the throat (pharynx) through the chest cavity and into the stomach.

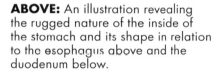

Esophagus

Gastro-esophageal junction

Stomach

Critical Sphincter *The gastro-esophageal junction (GOJ)— where the esophagus meets the stomach—is critical. Although on a macroscopic level there*

ABOVE: An illustration revealing the rugged nature of the inside of the stomach and its shape in relation to the esophagus above and the duodenum below.

isn't much to see, under the microscope the transition from the esophagus to the stomach becomes clear. The GOJ also functions as the lower esophageal sphincter, a device capable of constricting the lumen (space within a tube) to prevent the passage of substances along it. At the most basic level, the GOJ junction prevents food pouring out whenever you lean over to pick something up from the floor. More importantly, it also keeps the strong stomach acid within the stomach, which is designed to tolerate such an intense pH. When the lower esophageal sphincter leaks, even briefly, acid tracks along the esophagus resulting in damage to the esphageal epithelium and causing the sensation of pain. This is what's known as heartburn—nothing to do with the heart, but all about the esophagus.

How the Stomach Works

The stomach is a muscular reservoir responsible for the bulk of food breakdown, with just a little absorption. Stretch receptors from our stomach signal to our brain when we're full, while its ridged interior helps to pulverize food to allow the acid and enzymes to do their work. The resulting fluid is called chyme.

The acidity inside the stomach is phenomenal, thanks to the parietal cells that secrete hydrochloric acid to reach a pH of 1.8 to 3.5. (Normal body pH is between 7.35 and 7.45; car battery acid has a pH of around 1.) The enzyme responsible for this, the proton pump, transports hydrogen ions (H+) across the cell membrane against a concentration gradient of three million to one, the steepest ion gradient in the body. Not only does this strong acid help to digest food, it is also required to activate pepsin, a potent enzyme that breaks down protein into peptides and amino acids prior to absorption.

Why Doesn't the Stomach Digest Itself? *The stomach uses a variety of mechanisms to protect it from itself. First, there are the copious mucus secretions that coat the stomach lining. Second, the molecular design of the digestive enzymes protects the cells that produce them: They aren't activated until they leave the cell and enter the acidic environment of the stomach contents. And third, acid production is regulated so that it peaks only when required.*

Small breaches in these defenses can cause gradual erosion of the stomach wall, known as a peptic ulcer. Left untreated this can perforate, releasing acid and digestive enzymes into the abdomen.

What Are the Duodenum, Jejenum, and Ileum?

After the stomach, the food that has become chyme is released in limited amounts into the small intestine. The release is coordinated by the pyloric sphincter, a strong ring of muscle that encircles the junction between the stomach and small intestine. Such controlled release, modulated by feedback mechanisms relating to the fat content of the meal, allows for efficient digestion within the stomach. It also prevents flooding of the enzymes in the small intestine. The small intestine itself is divided into three distinct zones: the duodenum, the jejunum, and the ileum.

The Duodenum *This follows on from the pyloric sphincter of the stomach and receives secretions from the nearby pancreas and gallbladder. It's a relatively fixed organ whose prime purpose is to allow the copious bicarbonate ions found in the pancreatic secretions to counteract the fierce acid of the stomach.*

The Jejunum and the Ileum *The muscular movement of these mobile structures propels the nutrient-rich fluid along their length. It is in these parts of the bowel that the majority of nutrient absorption takes place.*

Villi *Finger-like fronds of tissue protrude into the lumen of the small intestine to increase its surface-area-to-volume ratio and facilitate absorption. Nutrients pass into the blood vessels that pass straight to the liver (the enterohepatic circulation) with the exception of digested fats, which pass instead to the lymphatic circulation.*

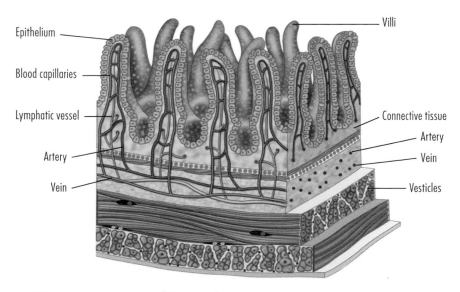

ABOVE: A cross-section of the small intestine.

The Pancreas

The pancreas is a knobbly, comet–shaped gland that sits high in the abdomen. Its head is cradled by the "C" shape of the duodenum, its body lies behind the stomach, and its tail stretches across to the left to brush against the spleen.

The pancreas has two different but important roles:

- *It works as an exocrine gland by secreting enzymes that break down proteins, fats, and complex carbohydrates in the chyme that leaves the stomach.*

- *It also functions as an endocrine gland, secreting hormones into the blood. These hormones include insulin, somatostatin, pancreatic polypeptide, and glucagon, and are produced by specialized cells in the Islets of Langerhans.*

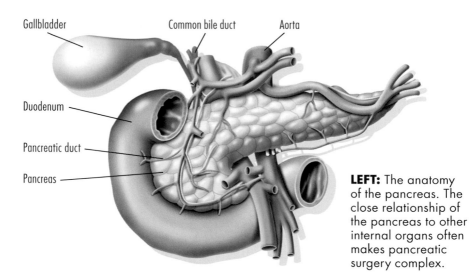

Gallbladder   Common bile duct   Aorta

Duodenum

Pancreatic duct

Pancreas

LEFT: The anatomy of the pancreas. The close relationship of the pancreas to other internal organs often makes pancreatic surgery complex.

What Does Insulin Do?

Insulin lowers blood sugar by stimulating cells in the liver, muscle, and fat (adipose tissue) to absorb glucose from the blood. Glucose functions as the main energy supply in the blood and excess glucose absorbed in this way is principally converted into an intracellular store of energy. In liver and muscle tissue, glucose is converted to glycogen. In adipose tissue it is converted to triglyceride fats.

Blood Sugar Control: Hyper– and Hypoglycemia *The body releases insulin as blood sugar rises, aiming to prevent it from exceeding a certain limit of concentration (4–8 mmol/L). At higher concentrations (hyperglycemia), glucose interferes with the fluid balance between the cells and the blood, drawing water from the cells through osmotic pressure and driving an unquenchable thirst as the body strives to maintain normal ranges within the bloodstream. Furthermore, despite all that glucose floating around in the blood, if cells can't access it, they still feel chemically "starved" and become unable to function as normal. This is what happens in the condition diabetes mellitus, when either no insulin is produced because the Islets of Langerhans have been destroyed (Type 1, sometimes called "childhood" diabetes) or very little insulin is produced and what little there is no longer works effectively (Type 2, sometimes called "late onset" diabetes).*

In Type 1 diabetes, where there is no insulin present at all, in desperation, the liver begins to break down fats and proteins in greater quantities to try to provide the body with some energy. This is only a short-term solution, however. Those metabolic processes release ketone bodies into the blood, causing ketoacidosis and creating further problems as the acid load increases.

Of course, problems arise if the body's blood sugar falls too low as well (hypoglycemia). Typically, as blood glucose falls, the production of insulin diminishes. Concurrently, the pancreas releases the hormone glucagon, which stimulates the liver to break down its glycogen stores and release glucose into the bloodstream. Hypoglycemia can result from an overdose of insulin, alcohol, or following periods of starvation.

✳ FACT

Steve Redgrave was diagnosed with diabetes in 1997. In 2000, in Sydney, he became the first athlete to win a gold medal at five consecutive Olympic Games. He's one of several professional athletes with diabetes mellitus.

The Liver: You Can't Live Without It

It's the largest gland in the body and you can't live without it. Soft and pliable, the liver sits beneath the diaphragm on the right-hand side of the abdomen, wrapping around the inferior vena cava and smothering itself onto the gallbladder. It is unusual in the body, because it has two separate blood supplies: the hepatic artery, which delivers oxygenated blood from the heart, and the hepatic portal vein, which delivers blood from the digestive tract for processing. One of the most incredible facts about the liver is that it can regenerate itself following surgery.

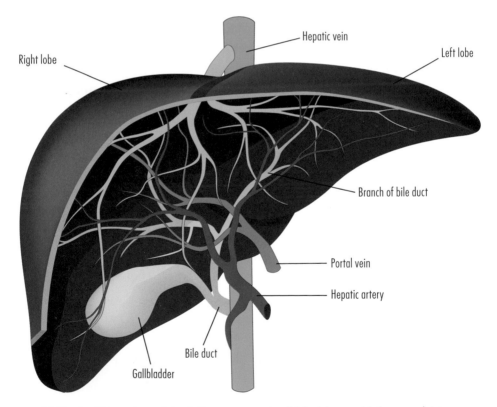

Hepatic vein

Right lobe

Left lobe

Branch of bile duct

Portal vein

Hepatic artery

Bile duct

Gallbladder

ABOVE: An illustration of the biliary system (gall bladder and bile vessels) in relation to the liver and its blood supply (the hepatic circulation).

Liver Function

The liver performs over five hundred different metabolic processes. Because of its huge importance as part of the digestive process and in the overall running of the human body, it has become one of the most transplanted organs worldwide, along with the kidneys and heart. The first liver transplant took place in 1963 in Colorado. However, subsequent survival rates were poor until the introduction of the immunosuppressant drug cyclosporin in the 1980s. Here are some of the liver's most important functions:

- *The production and secretion of bile (a green fluid of mucus, salts, water, and bilirubin, the pigment from hemoglobin breakdown). Bile drains through the bile ducts and is stored in the gallbladder. It aids the digestion of fat in the small intestine.*
- *The synthesis of clotting factors.*
- *Filters the blood and helps remove harmful bacteria and chemicals.*
- *Stores extra blood, which can be released quickly when needed.*
- *The conversion of glucose to glycogen as a short-term energy store.*
- *The breakdown of glycogen to release glucose into the blood as blood sugar falls.*
- *The synthesis of glucose (gluconeogenesis) from other substrates such as amino acids and other carbohydrates, as blood sugar falls and glycogen stores become exhausted.*
- *Mediating cholesterol metabolism (cholesterol synthesis, transport through the blood, and excretion into the bile).*
- *The storage of iron.*
- *The conversion of harmful ammonia into urea, which is then removed by the kidneys.*
- *The metabolism and clearance of many drugs, including alcohol.*
- *The synthesis of major plasma proteins, such as albumin.*
- *The storage of vitamins, minerals, and sugars.*
- *Breaks down and eliminates excess hormones.*
- *Helps maintain blood pressure.*

The Large Intestine

The role of the large intestine is to absorb water from food and drink, but also from the several quarts (liters) of digestive fluids secreted into the GI tract each day. Bacteria resident in the large intestine play an important part in the synthesis of Vitamin K, which is essential for clotting. Finally, all indigestible matter plus the waste products secreted by the liver are expelled from the body as feces.

Appendicitis

The appendix is a vestigial organ—that is, an organ that had an important role further back in evolution but that we no longer need. It arises from the cecum—a pouch at the beginning of the large intestine. When the appendix becomes blocked, inflammation occurs and this becomes appendicitis. Left untreated, there is a risk that the appendix will perforate (burst) releasing infected fecal matter into the abdomen and inducing septic shock.

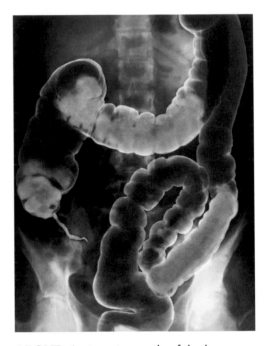

ABOVE: An imaging study of the large bowel and appendix. The appendix is the narrow, wormlike structure seen in pink to the left of the image.

FACT

The intestines convert excreted bilirubin—the pigment in bile that comes from hemoglobin breakdown—into stercobilin. That is the pigment responsible for the brown color of feces.

Sports Nutrition

Nutrition itself has become a hot topic over the last few decades. As a population, the world has better access to food and dietary education than ever before. Yet despite this, eating disorders and malnutrition persist and, in the case of the obesity epidemic, are even increasing. Sports nutrition follows the same principles as all good nutrition: to provide enough energy to meet the required needs without harmful excess, and to provide vital substances that the body cannot produce itself. A healthy and balanced diet should negate the need for vitamin and mineral supplements in healthy adults most of the time, even for elite athletes. And it might be of some interest to learn that not all fats are bad. Nutritionists recommend that between 20 and 30 percent of our energy intake should come from fats. Fats are essential for cell membranes and for the absorption of fat-soluble vitamins A, D, and E.

The Pre-event Meal

The last meal before a major sporting event is known to influence performance. While experts stress that it cannot compensate for a poor training diet, they do offer some guidance:

- *The pre-event meal should focus on carbohydrate intake, since this is the food group most easily broken down into glucose (the unit of energy currency in the body) and converted into glycogen (the energy store in the liver and muscles that's most efficiently converted back to glucose during the event).*

- *A small meal (four to five hundred calories) can be eaten two to three hours before the event. Large meals, or those involving protein and fat, may need a period of up to six hours to avoid gastrointestinal distress. Carbonated drinks are discouraged as the volume of gas can interfere with digestion.*

- *For early morning events, a carbohydrate-rich meal is recommended the night before, although high-fiber carbohydrates, such as beans and pulses should be avoided as they may cause intestinal discomfort.*

- *Hydration is paramount before, during, and after the event, but also throughout the training schedule.*

FACT

Amino acids are the molecular "building blocks" of protein. The human body can synthesize many amino acids itself. Those that it cannot synthesize are termed "essential amino acids." They include phenylalanine, valine, threonine, tryptophan, isoleucine, methionine, leucine, lysine, and histidine and need to be consumed in the diet.

Nutrition During Exercise

For events lasting longer than one hour, research has shown that consuming carbohydrates unequivocally extends endurance performance, provided that the carbohydrates are spread evenly across the event. This carbohydrate—usually in the form of a sports drink or gel—should be consumed evenly across the time period: Regular sips at fifteen to twenty minute intervals are more effective than a single bolus at the two hour mark. In order to optimize performance, current research suggests athletes should aim to replenish 0.7g of carbohydrate per kilogram of body weight for each hour of exercise in order to optimize performance.

THE SCIENCE OF SEX

9

It's All in the Genes

One of the most interesting things about the cycle of life is that, in a way, we all start out the same. As the sperm fertilizes the egg and the cells begin to divide, we all develop along the same path: ball of cells, disk of cells, cavities, bean-shaped outline, and so on. It is only as certain sex-linked genes become expressed that sexual differentiation becomes apparent. It is not until around week six that organs begin to move to their correct places (such as the descent of the testes) and various tubes and structures begin to settle down. It's this biological hesitancy within the womb that explains our reproductive anatomy, which is otherwise far from straightforward.

The Male Reproductive System

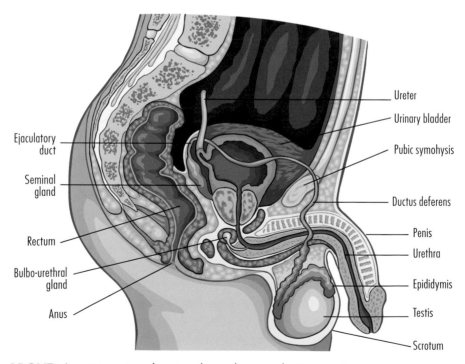

ABOVE: A cross-section showing the male reproductive anatomy .

The testes are the powerhouses of male reproduction: The interstitial cells of Leydig secrete the hormone testosterone into the blood and the seminiferous tubules produce sperm (spermatogenesis), which are then stored in the epididymis. The production of sperm begins during puberty and continues into old age. It takes about two and a half months to create each one, which then either leaves the body via ejaculation or dies within the scrotum, where it is consumed by macrophages (a type of white blood cell).

Semen contains both sperm and seminal plasma (the watery contributions from the prostate and seminal vesicles). This extra fluid includes fructose and vitamins for nourishment, as well as bicarbonate, enzymes, and minerals to help neutralize the acids encountered in the vagina.

Erection *Erection occurs as the arterioles supplying the cavernous and spongiosus bodies (corpus cavernosa and corpus spongiosum respectively) dilate, constricting the drainage of blood by the veins of the penis. This is mediated by the parasympathetic nervous system and can be influenced by the brain. The signal to ejaculate comes from the sympathetic nervous system and, once started, cannot be stopped.*

Testosterone *Healthy adult men produce testosterone at a steady rate of 10mg/day in response to a feedback mechanism orchestrated by the hypothalamus, which secretes gonadotropin-releasing hormone (GnRH), and the anterior pituitary, which secretes luteinizing hormone (LH) and follicle-stimulating hormone (FSH). Testosterone promotes libido, aggression, facial hair, enlargement of the larynx and vocal cords, increased muscle and bone growth, and increased red blood cell production. It's also essential for the production and release of sperm.*

Anabolic Androgenic Steroids

Anabolic androgenic steroids refer to synthetic versions of testosterone. They are taken because of the effects that they have on musculoskeletal physique and red blood cell production and have been trialed in various wasting diseases (such as HIV) to try to build up muscle bulk. They are also used to treat a clinical condition where the gonads (ovaries or testes) are not functioning fully (hypogonadism).

FACT

According to the World Health Organization (WHO), "sex" refers to the biological and physiological characteristics that define men and women. Gender, on the other hand, refers to the socially constructed roles, behaviors, activities, and attributes that society considers appropriate for men and women.

Their use, or rather abuse, for cosmetic and competitive reasons has been increasing since the 1950s. Yet their use carries a number of risks, depending on the type of synthetic product administered and the kind of testosterone function it mimics. Side effects include behavioral disturbances, blood clots and stroke from the raised red blood cell count, and the development of liver and heart disease. In women, they can induce the development of facial hair and male pattern baldness. In growing teens, they can lead to short stature from the premature fusion of the bones. Regular use can also lead to impotence and a reduction in testicular size and sperm count.

The Female Genitourinary Tract

In women, the ovaries are primarily responsible for reproductive health. They produce and release eggs (ova) and they secrete the female sex hormones estrogen and progesterone (along with a little testosterone). Like the testes, the ovaries are influenced by LH and FSH from the anterior pituitary gland, which in turn is affected by GnRH from the hypothalamus. Unlike the testes, the ovaries produce hormones on a cyclical rather than steady basis, as the lining of the uterus (endometrium) is primed for implantation each month.

Healthy women release one egg each month (between the menarche, when periods start at age nine to seventeen, until the menopause at age forty-five to fifty-five, when they stop). There is no pattern as to which ovary releases the egg, it occurs at random.

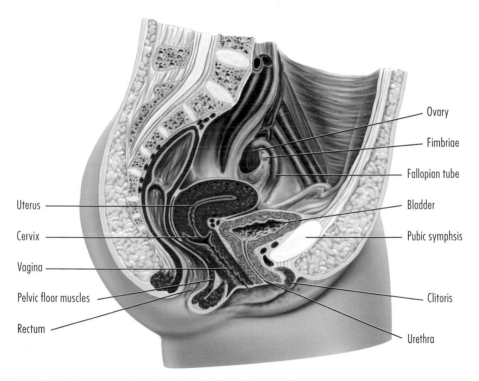

Uterus

Cervix

Vagina

Pelvic floor muscles

Rectum

Ovary

Fimbriae

Fallopian tube

Bladder

Pubic symphsis

Clitoris

Urethra

ABOVE: Cross-section showing the female reproductive anatomy.

Progesterone and Estrogen *Progesterone has a prominent role in preparing the body for pregnancy, both before and after fertilization. Estrogen also influences the development and secretion of the endometrium and mucosal folds of the oviducts, but it has other roles:*

- *It promotes fatty deposits in the breasts and buttocks to give the characteristic female outline.*
- *It stimulates bone growth, along with adrenal male sex hormones (androgens), and protects the body's calcium stores in the bones.*
- *Estrogen widens the pelvis and prompts the closure of the epiphyseal plates in long bones during puberty, leading to the shorter stature of women when compared to men.*

Is Sex Set in Stone?

The observation that many female characteristics result from the absence of androgens rather than through direct biological processes have led to the suggestion that "female" is the default position for humans. At a genetic level, sex is determined by paired threads of genetic material inside each cell (chromosomes). Since women are XX, and one of each chromosome must come from each parent, it is the sperm that determines a child's sex. An X chromosome in the sperm produces a girl, while a Y chromosome in the sperm produces a boy.

Ovaries that Change to Testes *Up until week six, both male and female embryos look alike and the primitive version of both the ovaries and testes (the primordial gonad) is sexually bipotential. Once the Y chromosome is activated it leads to the production of H–Y antigen, which destroys the presumptive ovary and instead switches the development of the primordial gonad into the embryonic testes. The embryonic testes then produce testosterone as well as a substance called Mullerian Regression Factor (MRF). MRF acts to destroy the forerunners of the female internal genitalia; the absence of testosterone causes the primitive male internal genitalia to regress.*

Male or Female?

So, at what level are sex and gender determined? Female embryos with XX chromosomes can develop external male genitalia if they are exposed to high levels of androgens (most commonly through a tumor that leads to the condition congenital adrenal hyperplasia).

Conversely, male embryos with XY chromosomes can develop a female external appearance if their cells cannot respond to androgens (androgen insensitivity disorder). In these cases, the womb does not develop and the testes remain within the abdomen. Alternatively, a mixed picture can occur. Or everything can appear normal at birth with problems arising during puberty. At a biological level, gender does not appear to be clear cut. At a cultural and behavioral level, it is even less so.

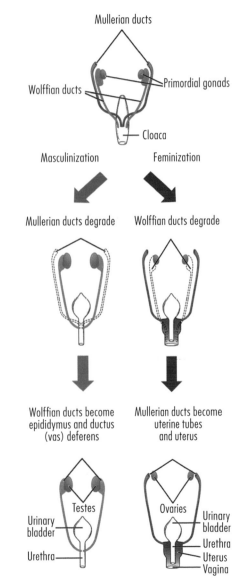

RIGHT: A diagram to show the progression from primordial gonad to male or female genitalia, depending on the presence or absence of the Y chromosome respectively.

Gender Verification in Competitive Sports

Men and women are separated in competitive sports. At first, classification was based on appearance. In the twentieth century, the discovery of the Barr body (the inactive X chromosome in women's somatic cells) led to the introduction of Barr body testing on samples taken from the mouths of females at the 1966 Olympics.

However, that doesn't fully answer the question, because if someone has a male genotype (XY) but a female phenotype (appearance)—due to androgen insensitivity—for example, they would fail the Barr body test, but would also lack any real advantage over female athletes. So is this classification that fair? And what of the reverse situation—women who live as women, but whose ambiguous sexual development leaves them with higher levels of testosterone or other male advantages?

Testosterone Assays *The latest proposal for sports verification involves performing testosterone assays and making allowances for those who have increased levels for medical reasons (such as congenital adrenal hyperplasia). Yet it is difficult to decide on a fair threshold, since some male Olympic athletes test within the female range and some women within the male range.*

✳ FACT

Some 500 male to female sex reassignment surgeries are performed each year. Some are performed on newborns with ambiguous genitalia; others on adults who believe they have the wrong genitalia for their gender.

The Genetic Lottery *Some argue that women who have naturally occurring high levels of testosterone should be able to benefit from the fact. After all, athletes with naturally occurring tall statures frequently benefit from their luck in the genetic lottery! It's a complicated question. But then so many questions of gender are.*

10
THE LIFE CYCLE

When Does Life Begin?

This question has dogged philosophers for years and we still don't have a concrete answer: When does life begin? Is it at birth? If so, at what stage? Is it when a fetus is capable of surviving in the outside world? Is it at the point of fertilization? Or later, when the floating ball of cells separates into those that will form the placenta (and ultimately be thrown away) and those that will form the child (cherished for the rest of his or her life)?

Given that the energy supplies for the cell (mitochondria) have their own DNA and are passed directly from the egg of the mother to the child—with no genetic change at all—is it even possible to question whether our life begins at all? Is each one of us simply a continuation of our mother's DNA with a paternal contribution to spice things up? Or are the answers to all of these questions simply beyond our understanding?

Fertilization

While actually a multistep process, fertilization is the point at which new genetic material is combined within a single cell for the first time. Given the right environment, that single cell (the fertilized egg) can go on to produce a new person and begin a new life. Of the three hundred million or so sperm released in the ejaculate, only a few hundred will reach the egg (ovum)—but, of course, it only takes one sperm for fertilization to occur.

A single, fully mature sperm (spermatozoon) consists

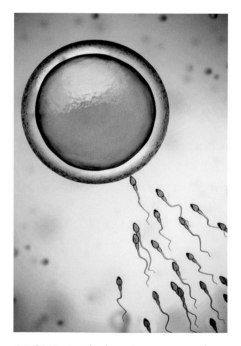

ABOVE: Just before the moment of fertilization.

of a head that contains the genetic material, a cap (the acrosome), and a wavy, motile tail (flagellum). In the flagellum, nine pairs of peripheral microtubules surround two central ones, and it is the contraction of these microtubules that provides the sperm's characteristic swimming motion.

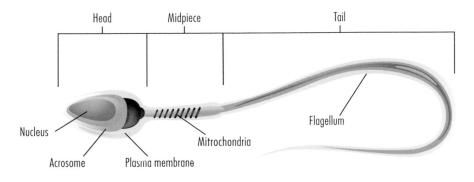

ABOVE: Anatomy of a spermatozoon.

While the sperm focuses on delivering genetic material, the ovum must also nourish the young embryo before implantation occurs. At ovulation, a jelly-like substance—the zona pellucida—surrounds the ovum and a layer of follicular cells—the corona radiata—surround that to further support the egg's nutritional requirements. Upon reaching the egg, the spermatozoon releases its acrosomal enzymes to separate the follicular cells and pass through the zona pellucida. It binds to the egg membrane, allowing the ovum to engulf the entire head and tail of the sperm. What stops multiple spermatozoa from entering the egg? As soon as one enters, a chemical reaction takes place in the zona pellucida that blocks access to the rest. The ovum completes the final stage of cell division for sexual reproduction (meiosis) to leave twenty-three maternal chromosomes that bind with the twenty-three carried in the sperm. The combined forty-six chromosomes thus complete the human complement of genetic material and the egg is considered fertilized.

The Young Embryo

Zygote is the term used for the single cell that results from fertilization. It divides and divides and divides again (cellular proliferation) until it resembles a berry (morula). By the time the zygote becomes a morula—approximately four days—it has traveled along the Fallopian tube to the uterus. This homogenous collection of cells now begins to differentiate into an inner cell mass with a peripheral sheet of cells (the trophoblast). At this stage, the bundle of cells is called a blastocyst: The trophoblast, which contains a cavity, will later grow into the placenta and amniotic sack, while the inner cell mass will become the embryo.

Implantation occurs at around day six to seven, and the endometrium completely envelops the embryo. The embryonic period lasts one to eight weeks, after which the embryo becomes a fetus. Most major organs form between weeks four and eight,

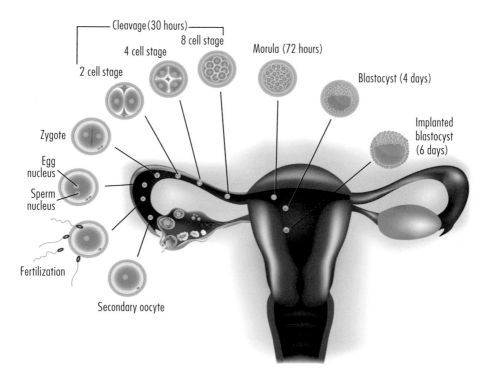

ABOVE: This is how we all begin: the first few steps following fertilization.

making this the most critical phase in terms of exposure to drugs and other substances that harm the developing embryo. The primitive heart starts beating at around five weeks. During the second and third trimesters, development is chiefly characterized by fetal growth.

Anatomical Changes for Living Underwater

Clearly, from the moment of birth, a baby must be able to breathe air. Yet in utero, the fetus receives all its nutrients (oxygen, glucose, and more) through transport across the placenta and lives entirely surrounded by amniotic fluid. In addition to the placenta and umbilical cord, a growing fetus has a number of adaptations that fit its underwater existence.

First of all, it conserves energy by developing lungs at a relatively late stage. After all, it only needs them for life on the outside. Instead, its blood shunts from the left side of the heart to the right via an oval hole (foramen ovale) encouraged by the high resistance of the fetal pulmonary vascular bed. The little blood that does make its way into the pulmonary artery is diverted away from the lungs by a channel called the ductus arteriosus, which leads straight to the aorta. Finally, blood flow to the liver is reduced (as the maternal liver has already processed substances ingested from outside). Instead, half the circulation bypasses the liver through the ductus venosus, which drains straight into the inferior vena cava (which drains straight into the heart).

Hole in the Heart Babies *At birth, the expansion of the lungs should alter the pressures within the heart and lead to closure of the foramen ovale. If this does not occur, blood is still shunted away from the lungs. Without the placenta, the baby cannot meet its oxygen requirements and emergency medical intervention is required.*

What the Placenta Does

The placenta is a domed structure that acts as the lungs, the liver, and the digestive tract of a growing fetus. It allows the transfer of substances from the maternal blood to the fetal blood and vice versa, in order to supply essential nutrients (glucose, oxygen, amino acids) and to remove waste products (carbon dioxide, lactate). It also transports immunoglobulin (immune response) antibodies and drugs such as caffeine and alcohol. Amniotic fluid surrounds the growing fetus, cushioning it from blows from the outside and helping the fetus to develop its swallowing mechanism. Fetal urine also appears in the fluid itself.

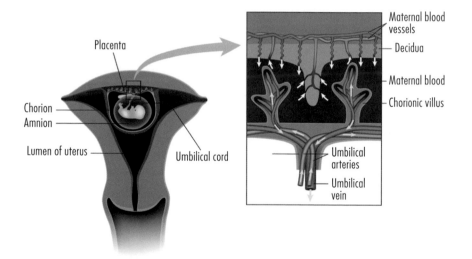

ABOVE: Placenta function: A close-up cross-section of the placenta (right) shows the direction of transfer of vital substances and waste.

FACT

Many mammals, even herbivores, eat the nutritious afterbirth of their young. In recent years, placentophagy in humans has hit the headlines as a way to avoid postnatal depression, although the medical world rejects this view.

Growing Babies

There's more to pregnancy than growing a bump and dealing with hemorrhoids and hormones. The placenta produces a hormone called relaxin that causes widespread relaxation of ligaments while the effects of progesterone increase the "leakiness" of capillaries causing swelling (edema). The pubic and pelvic (sacroiliac) joints widen in preparation for the passage of the baby's head through the birth canal at delivery.

Almost every system of the mother's body is affected, from cardiac output (which increases by 40 percent after only three months) to the composition of blood (increased platelets and white blood cells among others) to the tidal volume of the lungs, which decrease. The esophageal sphincter relaxes, causing reflux, and the glomerular filtration rate at the kidney increases. Even hair growth changes, as progesterone halts natural hair loss, which then returns with some dramatic flair a few months after delivery.

Childbirth

A few days before birth, progesterone levels drop in the maternal blood allowing unopposed estrogen to increase the excitability of the uterine smooth muscle. Sensory receptors on the cervix detect the pressure of the fetal head and stimulate the hypothalamus and posterior pituitary gland to release oxytocin. This peptide hormone causes powerful uterine contractions, propelling the fetus through the birth canal (cervix and vagina).

The first stage of labor begins with the onset of contractions and the dilation of the cervix—this may last for many hours. Eventually, with stronger and more regular contractions, this moves into the active phase, during which time the cervix softens and dilates fully. It is in the first stage of labor that a woman will most likely experience the rupture of membranes (ROM). As the baby's head descends into the pelvis, it separates the fluids, creating the forewaters in front of the head and hindwaters surrounding the body. The amniotic sac within the womb then breaks, expelling the amniotic fluid through the cervix and out of the vagina.

The transition period comes with the dilation of the cervix to about 4 inches (10 cm). This marks the onset of stage two, in which powerful contractions begin and a woman will experience the urge to push, due to pressure low in the pelvis. The contractions then work to move the baby down the birth canal for delivery. Further contractions separate the placenta from the uterine wall and it is expelled.

Recovery *While pelvic floor exercises and gentle walking can commence within hours of delivery, more strenuous activity is not recommended following childbirth. Ligaments and joints need to become less stretchy and tears should be given time to heal first.*

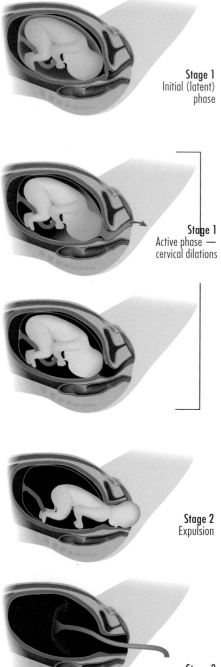

Stage 1
Initial (latent)
phase

Stage 1
Active phase —
cervical dilations

Stage 2
Expulsion

Stage 3
Delivery
of placenta

RIGHT: The three stages of labor: active phase, expulsion of the baby, and delivery of the placenta.

11

MICROSCOPIC
ANATOMY

Genetics

The question of biological inheritance has haunted human history for centuries: Wars have been fought, empires won and lost, and execution warrants signed over the issue. The discovery of the structure of DNA in the mid-twentieth century revolutionized our knowledge on the subject and launched a brand new scientific discipline: genetics.

What Is DNA?

DNA stands for deoxyribonucleic acid, a name so cumbersome that it risks alienating everyone right from the start. Yet its structure, and the elegant way in which it encodes the blueprint for life on Earth, makes it one of the most fascinating pieces of microscopic anatomy discovered to date.

Found in almost all living cells, DNA forms a double helix, much like a ladder that twists around itself. Its "rungs" are comprised of base pairs of nucleic acids, and it is the sequence of those base pairs that differentiates one human from the next—and from chimpanzees, slugs, snails, and seaweed. During day-to-day cell function, the ladder "unzips" in segments to allow other pieces of the cell's apparatus to access sections of the code and to carry out vital cell functions.

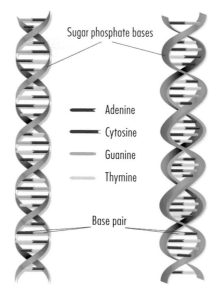

Sugar phosphate bases

— Adenine

— Cytosine

— Guanine

— Thymine

Base pair

By unzipping the ladder completely—splitting the DNA molecule into two separate halves—and combining it with a DNA strand from someone else, it is possible to create a new person. This is the molecular basis of sexual reproduction.

ABOVE: The structure of deoxyribonucleic acid (DNA).

Chromosomes

Human DNA is arranged into forty-six chromosomes: twenty-two pairs of autosomal chromosomes and one pair of sex chromosomes. The sex chromosomes are labeled X and Y. Women have two X chromosomes; men have one X and one Y.

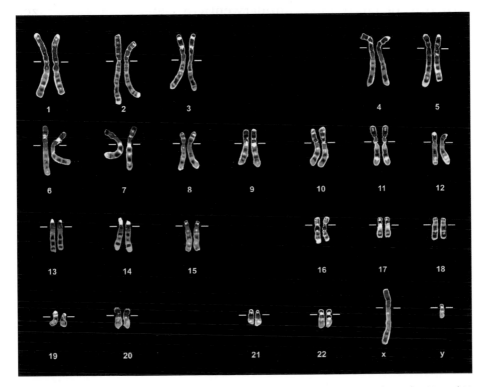

ABOVE: The full complement of male human chromosomes: note how the X and Y chromosomes differ in size and quantity of genetic material.

FACT

Although men are often taller, stronger, and faster than their female counterparts, they actually have less DNA. The Y chromosome is shorter, lacking genetic material and making men more susceptible to certain inherited diseases such as hemophilia and Duchenne's muscular dystrophy.

Gene Therapy

Since scientists discovered that single gene defects could cause devastating diseases, the prospect of gene therapy has become something of a Holy Grail in the medical profession. Early efforts focused on conditions caused by a single mutation, such as cystic fibrosis, muscular dystrophy, sickle cell anemia, and certain types of hemophilia.

Gene therapy generally focuses on using viruses to introduce new DNA into cells. Since viruses routinely "hijack" cell machinery to produce viral DNA, they would seem the natural choice as a means of transmitting artificial DNA into the patient. Scientists add the therapeutic DNA into the virus in the lab and then "infect" the patient with the altered virus. The viral "hijack" then results in expression of the therapeutic DNA.

"Somatic" gene therapy refers to altering the non-sex-cell DNA of a person. Any changes induced will stay within that individual. "Germ line" cell therapy, however, involves changing the DNA of the sex cells. Such changes will then be passed on to future generations. Unsurprisingly, this latter group has attracted more discussion and ethical debate and is currently banned in a number of countries.

FACT

The first successful case of human gene therapy was reported in 1990 when four-year-old Ashanti DeSilva received temporary relief from her inherited immunodeficiency. Doctors took blood from the patient and replaced a defective gene, which when introduced back into the bloodstream produced the crucial enzyme that she lacked.

Cloning

Cloning refers to the creation of a genetically identical organism. It occurs naturally in bacteria, plants, and insects as part of asexual reproduction. In humans, it is responsible for the natural formation of identical twins. Artificial human cloning, however, is not yet possible nor is it considered ethical by most of the scientific community. The arrival of Dolly the sheep in 1996 highlighted that it was possible to take an adult cell, implant it into an egg (ovum), implant that into a primed uterus, and generate a brand new life with identical genetic material to the adult mammal. However, the outcome did not come easily: 277 eggs resulted in only twenty-nine embryos. These produced just three lambs at birth, of which only one survived (Dolly).

ABOVE: Perhaps the most famous ovine ever, Dolly the sheep was the world's first cloned mammal.

Inside the Cell

The cell is the smallest functional unit of an organism. It has a nucleus that contains DNA, a cell membrane, and the gel–like fluid within (cytoplasm). In the cytoplasm are other pieces of cellular apparatus (organelles). These include the Golgi apparatus, which packages and secretes proteins and ribosomes. Ribosomes translate messenger ribonucleic acid (mRNA) into amino acids, the building blocks of protein. The rough endoplasmic reticulum (RER) is a concertina–like folded membranous sack that is studded with ribosomes. The smooth endoplasmic reticulum, meanwhile, concerns itself more with lipid (fat) and carbohydrate metabolism.

Lysosomes function as the waste disposal system of the cell, as well as providing a "patch" to cover any holes that appear in the cell membrane. Centrioles are microtubules that help provide structure during cell division. Finally, there are the powerhouses of the cell: the mitochondria.

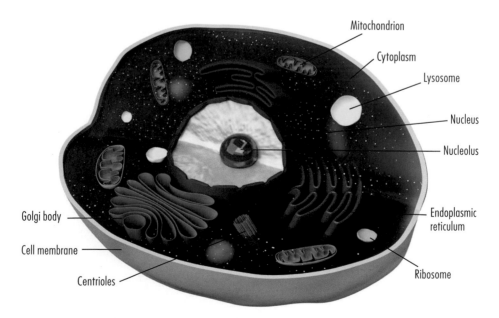

ABOVE: Inside the cell. This cutaway diagram of an animal cell reveals the makeup of the cell and its various organelles.

The Cell's Powerhouse

Mitochondria (singular, mitochondrion) play a key role in oxidative phosphorylation, the process by which cells convert glucose into ATP (the energy currency of the body). Mitochondria have an outer membrane and an inner membrane, the latter wrinkled into characteristic crevices called christae. These wrinkles or christae form the site for the electron transport chain, a series of chemical reactions that drives protons (H+) across the inner membrane to create a powerful electrochemical gradient. The enzyme ATP-synthase then taps into this gradient to source the energy needed to fuse ADP with phosphate to create ATP.

Despite all the long words, oxidative phosphorylation is the most efficient way of converting glucose into energy that cells can use. It is, however, oxygen dependent. Without oxygen, the cell has a backup plan known as anaerobic respiration. This produces less ATP per glucose molecule consumed, as well as generating lactate, which enters the blood as lactic acid.

Lactic Acid Threshold *The switch from predominantly aerobic to predominantly anaerobic respiration has long been a subject of fascination for endurance athletes as well as lesser mortals who "feel the burn" while exercising. Along with VO_2max, the concept of lactate threshold training has also gained momentum in recent years as a way of maximizing endurance performance.*

Lactic acid threshold refers to the intensity of exercise at which there is an abrupt increase in blood lactate levels. It is too simplistic to say that this is the point at which respiration switches from aerobic to anaerobic, but a shift in their relative balance—or the body's ability to deal with lactate—does seem to occur.

Hidden Anatomy: What We Don't Yet Know

Our knowledge of macroscopic anatomy reached a plateau with the widespread acceptance of human dissection a few centuries ago. The arrival of the microscope revolutionized our understanding of cellular and subcellular structures.

New Frontiers

Biochemistry, genetics, and neuroscience continue to push back the frontiers of what we know about how we are put together and how we work. Our pursuit of microscopic anatomical knowledge is also directed at the study of disease. Be it stem cell therapy to treat spinal disorders, gene therapy to combat cancer, or electrical ablation to tackle heart disease, it is clear that the realms of what we don't yet know about anatomy offer hope for the future.

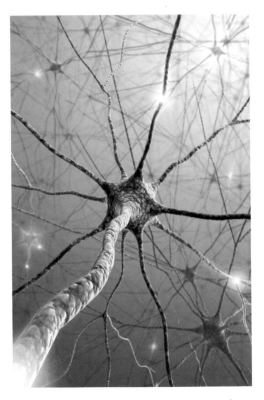

ABOVE: A close-up of a neural network—the latest frontier?

All in the Mind?

We still understand so little about what our body does each and every day without our even thinking about it. The rise of psychology as a scientific discipline attempts to understand our behavioral choices, closing the gap between structural molecular biology and neuroscience and the key philosophical questions that apply to us all.

Glossary

androgen A broad term covering the steroid hormones (natural and synthetic) that cause the development of male sex characteristics.

antibody A Y-shaped protein that binds to antigens on foreign targets as part of the immune system; also known as an immunoglobulin.

antidiuretic A substance that reduces the production of urine (diuresis).

antigen A substance that causes the immune system to generate antibodies against it—typically, a toxin or protein found on the cell wall of a microorganism.

bacteria Microscopic single-celled organisms whose DNA is loose within the cytoplasm rather than bound in the nucleus.

bile A green fluid of mucus, salts, water, and bilirubin (the pigment from hemoglobin breakdown).

cadaver A dead body used in dissection for the purpose of furthering medical education.

callus A thickened and hardened area of the body. Can occur in the skin following repetitive use or in bones as part of the healing process after fractures.

chemoreceptor Can refer to the cell or the receptor itself that is responsible for responding to changes in the chemical environment around it.

cholesterol A sterol compound required for cell membrane function and the synthesis of steroid hormones; thought to play a major role in the development of narrowing of arteries (atherosclerosis) and heart disease.

chromosome An X-shaped package of DNA, RNA, and scaffolding proteins. Humans have forty-six chromosomes (twenty-two standard (somatic) pairs, and one pair of sex chromosomes, X and Y).

congenital A condition that someone is born with. This may or may not be an inherited disorder.

electrical ablation Using electrical energy to destroy tissue that is conducting electricity abnormally within the heart.

electrolyte A substance that forms charged particles (ionizes) when dissolved in a fluid (solvent). Common physiological electrolytes are sodium chloride, potassium chloride, and calcium chloride, which ionize into sodium, potassium, calcium, and, of course, chloride ions in the blood.

enzyme Large molecules that selectively help (catalyze) chemical reactions within the body.

fibrin A non-globular protein that forms long, thin strands during the process of clotting.

fibronectin A high-molecular-weight glycoprotein involved in wound healing and embryonic development.

fontanelle Membrane covered opening between bone found in the skulls of infants.

gene A sequence of DNA in a specific location on a chromosome that codes for a specific characteristic in an organism—the molecular unit of heredity.

glucagon A hormone produced by the pancreas that increases blood sugar levels.

hematoma A localized collection of blood outside the blood vessels but within the body.

hormone Chemicals secreted into the blood that have a wide range of regulatory functions on other structures in the body.

hyperglycemia Blood sugar level above the normal range.

hyperthermia Core body temperature above the normal range.

hypoglycemia Blood sugar level below the normal range.

hypothermia Core body temperature below the normal range.

immunosuppressant A substance that subdues the reaction of the immune response. Often, but not exclusively, drugs used to treat autoimmune disease (where the body's immune system attacks itself).

islets of Langerhans The regions of the pancreas responsible for secreting endocrine hormones; named after the anatomist who first discovered them.

laminin An important protein in the basal lamina of the basement membrane (a supporting matrix beneath the epithelium).

macroscopic Visible without magnifying devices.

motor nerves Nerves that supply muscles.

neuron The functional unit of the nervous system.

phlegm A viscous substance secreted by the respiratory passages in response to inflammation; once believed to be one of the four essential body humors in ancient Greece.

photoreceptor A cell that responds to changes in levels of light; found in the retina.

platelet Cell fragments (from megakaryocytes) involved in clotting.

sagittal section A cross-section through the sagittal plane (the plane running from the nose to the back of the head that bisects the spine).

sensory nerves Nerves that transmit signals relating to sensory information.

steroid Organic chemical compound with four characteristic cycloalkane rings. The term is often applied to products that mimic the body's steroid hormones (typically the corticosteroids but also testosterone, aldosterone, progesterone, etc).

substrate Typically the substance upon which an enzyme acts.

suture A fixed, immovable junction between two bony edges. Also a process of joining two body tissues together through sewing (the term can also be applied to the thread used to perform this).

synapse Junction between two neurons.

thermoreceptor Receptor or neuron that carries the receptor that responds to changes in temperature.

tourniquet A device used to apply pressure around the arm or leg to restrict the flow of blood in the limb.

virus An infective agent that can typically only reproduce within the cell of the host; too small to be seen by standard light microscopy and consists of nucleic acids within a protein coat.

For More Information

American Academy of Arts & Sciences
136 Irving Street
Cambridge, MA 02138
Website: http://www.amacad.org
This organization supports research and scholarship in the sciences, offers fellowship programs for scientific thinkers, and sponsors lectures, discussions, and meetings about science topics around the United States.

American Association for the Advancement of Science (AAAS)
1200 New York Avenue NW
Washington, DC 20005
(202) 326-6400
Website: http://www.aaas.org
The AAAS advances communication among scientists and the public and encourages integrity in the sciences. It also promotes education in science and technology and international cooperation.

McGill Medical Museum
3775 University Street, Room B4
Montreal, QC H3A 2B4
Canada
(514) 398-7192 ext. 00838
Website: http://www.museevirtuel-virtualmuseum.ca
The museum displays artifacts that document the study and practice of medicine at McGill University and other teaching hospitals.

Museum of Health Care at Kingston
Ann Baillie Building National Historic Site

32 George Street
Kingston, ON K7L 2V7
Canada
(613) 548-2419
Website: http://www.museumofhealthcare.ca
This Canadian museum teaches the story of health and medicine
   in the country and explains how people have managed
   disease throughout history.

Museum of Science
1 Science Park
Boston, MA 02114
(617) 723-2500
Website: http://www.mos.org
This museum has a Hall of Life exhibit area that teaches people
   about human biology and includes seventy interactive
   exhibits.

The New York Academy of Sciences
7 World Trade Center
250 Greenwich Street, 40th Floor
New York, NY 10007-2157
(800) 843-6927
Website: http://www.nyas.org
This academy has been encouraging the study of the sciences
   for more than 200 years. It supports scientific research and
   literacy and provides scientific information via eBriefings
   and podcasts. Its New York City Science Education Initiative
   supports after-school mentoring of middle and high school
   students in the sciences.

U.S. National Library of Medicine (NLM)
8600 Rockville Pike

Bethesda, MD 20894
(888) 346-594-5983
Website: http://www.nlm.nih.gov
The NLM is part of the National Institutes of Health. It provides
   the public with information about the history of medicine,
   medical procedures, and health.

Websites

Because of the changing nature of Internet links, Rosen
Publishing has developed an online list of websites related to
the subject of this book. This site is updated regularly. Please
use this link to access the list:

http://www.rosenlinks.com/GCM/Anat

For Further Reading

Brynie, Faith Hickman. *101 Questions about Muscles*. Rev. ed. E-book. Minneapolis, MN: Twenty-First Century Books, 2013.

Claybourne, Anna. *The Usborne Complete Book of the Human Body*. London, UK: Usborne Publishing, Ltd., 2013.

Cracknell, James. *Body Science: The Head-to-Toe Guide to the Science in You*. New York, NY: DK Publishing, 2009.

Davies, Gill. *The Illustrated Timeline of Medicine* (History Timelines). New York, NY: Rosen Publishing, 2012.

Guttman, Burton, Anthony Griffiths, David Suzuki, and Tara Cullis. *Genetics: The Code of Life* (Contemporary Issues). New York, NY: Rosen Publishing, 2011.

Hollar, Sherman, ed. *A Closer Look at Biology, Microbiology, and the Cell* (Introduction to Biology). New York, NY: Britannica Educational Publishing and Rosen Educational Services, 2012.

Merino, Noel. *Human Genetics* (Current Controversies). Farmington Hills, MI: Greenhaven Press, 2010.

Rifkin, Benjamin A., and Michael J. Ackerman. *Human Anatomy: From the Renaissance to the Digital Age*. New York, NY: Harry N. Abrams, 2006.

Rogers, Kara, ed. *Bone and Muscle: Structure, Force, and Motion* (The Human Body). New York, NY: Britannica Educational Publishing and Rosen Educational Services, 2011.

Rogers, Kara, ed. *Blood* (The Human Body). New York, NY: Britannica Educational Publishing and Rosen Educational Services, 2011.

Rogers, Kara, ed. *The Digestive System* (The Human Body). Britannica Educational Publishing and Rosen Educational Services, 2011

Rogers, Kara, ed. *The Eye* (The Human Body). New York, NY: Britannica Educational Publishing and Rosen Educational Services, 2011.

Rogers, Kara, ed. *Medicine and Healers Through History* (Health and Disease in Society). New York, NY: Britannica Educational Publishing and Rosen Educational Services, 2011.

Rogers, Kara, ed. *The Reproductive System* (The Human Body). New York, NY: Britannica Educational Publishing and Rosen Educational Services, 2011.

Snedden, Robert. *Understanding the Brain and the Nervous System* (Understanding the Human Body). New York, NY: Rosen Publishing, 2010.

Sullivan, Robert. *Digestion and Nutrition* (The Human Body: How It Works). New York, NY: Chelsea House Publishers, 2009.

Walker, Pamela, and Elaine Wood. *Human Body Experiments* (Facts On File Science Experiments). New York, NY: Facts On File, 2010.

Wanjie, Anne, ed. *The Basics of the Human Body* (Core Concepts). New York, NY: Rosen Publishing, 2013.

Ward, Brian. *The Story of Medicine* (A Journey Through History). New York, NY: Rosen Publishing, 2012.

Index

Picture credits

The publishers would like to thank the following for permission to reproduce images.

Getty Images: pp. 86 (Stocktrek Images), 92 (BSIP/UIG)

iStock: pp. 23 (nicoolay), 43 (Ben-Schonewille), 44, 56 (cornishman), 78 (Eraxion)

Photolibrary: p. 47

Science Photo Library: pp. 6, 11 (Dr. Robert Friedland), 63 (Omikron), 76 (Claus Lunau), 96 (Alain Pol, ISM), 117 (Sovereign, ISM), 119 (Gustoimages)

Shutterstock: pp. 3, 5, 13, 27, 41, 51, 61, 71, 87, 99, 107, 115 (malexandric), 9 (Janaka Dharmasena), 21, 24, 34, 40, 91, 112, 114 (Alila Medical Media), 22 (Sebastian Kaulitzki), 29, 31 (Hein Nouwens), 32 (Yoko Design), 35, 36 (stihii), 52 (SARANS), 53, 116 (Designua), 57 (Antonio Abrignani), 58, 62, 65 (Alex Luengo), 59 (Convit), 67, 84 (snapgalleria), 72, 100 (Oguz Aral), 80 (Juan Gaertner), 88, 110 (GRei), 89 (Lightspring), 94 (Yoko Design), 103 (leonello calvetti), 108 (koya979), 109 (BlueRingMedia), 120 (eranicle), 122 (ktsdesign)

Wikimedia Commons: pp. 7 (tag PD-1923), 10 (tag PD-1923), 18 (InvictaHOG) 46 left, 46 right (John M. Harlow, M.D. tag PD-US), 48 (RazerM), 66 (BruceBlaus), 68 (Chabacano), 69, 105 (OpenStax College)

Jason Munro (illustrator): pp. 16, 17, 74